P9-DDD-870

We want to be thankful for our life . . . but comparison so easily steals this perspective from us. That's why I'm so thankful Nicki steps right into our most vulnerable places with practical ways to regain our confidence while also celebrating the success of those around us. *Why Her?* is the resource we all need to love the unique calling we've been handpicked for by God Himself.

Lysa TerKeurst, *New York Times* best-selling author and president of Proverbs 31 Ministries

This book is simply amazing. I love how Nicki Koziarz can weave the stories of her experiences with the tale of two sisters, Leah and Rachel, like no other. Simply a must-read for every woman, especially if you have listened to the lies in your own head that you don't measure up. Stop the comparison struggle and learn how you alone are loved and wonderful, just the way God made you to be.

Kelly C., *Why Her* focus group participant

She's funnier than me. I wish I were as smart as she is. If I were just as trim as she is. Confession: all those thoughts have run through my mind! The comparison trap is so, so easy to fall into. And, I know I'm not alone in this; most women get caught in the comparison trap. That's why I'm really grateful Nicki is tackling this topic in such an honest, real-life way. She makes you feel safe if you struggle with this and she gives you practical, biblical ways to get free and live with confidence instead of comparisons.

Jennifer Rothschild, best-selling author and speaker

I have lived so many of my years unconsciously asking the "why her?" question. Nicki Koziarz helped me see how that one question has shaped so many decisions in my life. I recommend this book to every woman—because all of us, at one time or another, have struggled with comparison. Reading this book had me shaking my head in agreement, tilting my head in "hmmm . . . ," and bowing my head in praise! Read this book . . . and discover how you can stop comparing yourself to her.

Anita F., *Why Her* focus group participant

I know firsthand how comparison can be a joy-killer. Nicki offers practical ways to identify and defeat comparison, pulling it out by its roots once and for all. I also love how Nicki reminds us to champion others' successes and genuinely love like Christ does. I will definitely use this book as a resource for when I am tempted to answer the call of comparison and unworthiness.

> **Candace Payne**, author of *Laugh It Up: Embrace Freedom and Experience Defiant Joy*, speaker, and viral video star

The title of Nicki's book, *Why Her?* is a question I have often asked myself. Nicki's words helped me to learn how to conquer all the ugliness that comparison can bring to my soul. Her words and truths were practical and biblically based. I will use these truths to overcome the lies of comparison and to bring greater peace to my soul. This is a book women of all ages should read and take to heart.

> **Julie W.**, *Why Her* focus group participant

Nicki covers a topic I believe many people struggle with but are ashamed to admit: Comparison. *Why Her?* takes an honest look at the comparison struggle and uncovers all of those not-so-pretty feelings we deal with. Nicki gives us personal and relatable stories from her past and dissects the struggle between two well-known sisters of the Bible. Most importantly, she also gives us strategies to overcome these feelings and encourages us to be the best us that God has created us to be.

> **Kathi Lipp**, best-selling author and speaker

WHY HER?

6 Truths We Need to Hear When Measuring Up Leaves Us Falling Behind

Nicki Koziarz

PUBLISHING GROUP

NASHVILLE, TENNESSEE

Copyright © 2018 by Nicki Koziarz
All rights reserved.
Printed in the United States of America

978-1-4627-5088-7

Published by B&H Publishing Group
Nashville, Tennessee

Dewey Decimal Classification: 248.843
Subject Heading: WOMEN \ SELF-IMPROVEMENT \
SELF-REALIZATION

Unless otherwise noted, all Scripture quotations are taken from the
Christian Standard Bible®, Copyright © 2017 by Holman Bible
Publishers. Used by permission. Christian Standard Bible® and CSB®
are federally registered trademarks of Holman Bible Publishers.

Also used: English Standard Version (ESV), copyright © 2001
by Crossway Bibles, a publishing ministry of Good News
Publishers. ESV Text Edition: 2007. All rights reserved.

Also used: Holy Bible, New International Version® (NIV),
copyright ©1973, 1978, 1984, 2011 by Biblica, Inc.®
Used by permission. All rights reserved worldwide.

Also used: New Living Translation (NLT), copyright ©
1996, 2004, 2007, 2013 by Tyndale House Foundation.
Used by permission of Tyndale House Publishers Inc.,
Carol Stream, Illinois 60188. All rights reserved.

Also used: The Message (MSG), copyright © 1993, 1994, 1995,
1996, 2000, 2001, 2002 by Eugene H. Peterson.

1 2 3 4 5 6 7 • 23 22 21 20 19 18

To my mom

the woman who taught me to
dance like no one is watching,
sing like no one is listening,
and do the things
only I can do.

Acknowledgments

BEHIND EVERY ONE OF THESE words is a faithful, loving, and kind husband. Kris Koziarz, you are a gift to me. Thank you for always believing in me, helping me sort through things, and giving me the space I need to do what I do. You're the best and I love this life God has given us together.

To my girls, Taylor, Hope, and Kennedy, you are a joy to be a momma to. Thank you for how gracious and understanding you were throughout the writing of this book. I'm so proud of you!

Lysa TerKeurst. I'll always give you the highest praise for your investment into my writing and speaking. It's a gift to have learned from the best. Thank you for being so generous in sharing your calling in a posture of leading others so they can learn from you.

Meredith Brock. You are by far the most supportive, caring, and go-getter woman I know. Thank you for pushing me, encouraging me, and representing me in all the things related to this project. You are one of the reasons I know God is good.

Melissa Taylor and the OBS team. I am forever grateful. Forever. I love this online community and each of you so much.

Proverbs 31 speakers, writers, and staff, WOW. What a team I get to be part of! You are all the wisest, godliest, and most creative people on the planet. I am so incredibly thankful for you.

Danya Jordan. One word: sparklers. Thank you. Just thank you.

B&H and Lifeway team. You guys are A-MAZING. Thank you for believing in this project and working so hard to make it happen.

Heather Nunn. Thank you for the prayers, kindness, and support you showed throughout the beginning stages of this book. You are a gift!

Lawrence. Thank you for your wisdom, guidance, and the big fancy words you brought into my life. I've learned so much from you, and it's been an honor to work with you.

David Abernathy. Your fingerprints are all over this project. Thank you for answering my gazillion questions and giving me insight about this story I would never have had without your help.

Holly M., Amy Lykins, Wendy P., Meg, Nichole Stern, Aunt Michelle, Karen C., Lisa Allen, Jen Schmidt, Kim Stewart, Whitney, Krista W., Shelly F., the *Why Her* focus group, and the countless others who prayed, processed, cheered, and encouraged me through this season, thank you. What a gift to have a community that cares.

And last but not least . . . to my dad. She's so proud of us. I know she is.

Contents

We Have to Start Here

AT SOME POINT IN THE core of every woman's soul, an ache begins to form. It starts with a glance or a glare, a conversation or a comment. It digs down deep into the wonder of our worth. But it ultimately takes the shape of a quiet question:

Why her?

Her, the neighbor. *Her*, the coworker. *Her*, the friend. *Her*, the sister. *Her*, the . . .

The competition.

Whoever she is, *her*.

"Why her?"

We don't dare ask this question out loud. Even addressing it in our journals is a no-no. It doesn't come up in our Bible study discussions.

We don't even want to admit we ever ask it. We shouldn't think such things. It's not nice.

But as we watch someone else living out what we desire most, and we don't quite feel like we're measuring up, we somehow can't seem to stop ourselves.

Why her?

What am I doing wrong?

What on earth is wrong with *me*?

As soon as we ask these questions, guilt consumes us. Why should it matter if *she* is so amazing, if *she* is so gorgeous, if *she* has so many nice things and can do it all so effortlessly? Yet for some reason, deep inside it still bothers us.

So we try to cover up the ache by making ourselves as impressive and put-together as *she* is. More to-dos. More striving. More makeup. More debt for more clothes. More perfect pictures on Instagram. We believe that surely somehow we can compensate for what's not enough about ourselves, compared to what's so incredible about *her*. But as much as we try to escape the comparison trap, we just can't.

Because . . .

She's there when we sit in meetings. Saying the witty things we wish we'd said. Sharing insights we wish we could see. Doing things we wish we could do.

She's there when we glance up and notice her behind us in the carpool line. The rearview mirror reflection reminds us what a great mom she is and how her hair roots are perfectly covered up every six weeks, while our roots end up looking like a skunk more weeks than not.

She's there in our minds late at night after a discouraging day. When disappointment distracts our thoughts. When we're angry at our circumstances. We lie there imagining how easy life is probably treating her tonight. Over there at her perfect house on Perfect Lane, with her perfect family, in her perfect world.

She's always there.

This threat of comparison isn't going away. I wish we could magically wake up tomorrow with an inner oomph that completely eliminates all our reasons for comparing. Instead, we'll likely be waking up to comparison shouts like these . . .

"Good morning, working woman—this is the day your low sales numbers get reported in that stand-up, pat-me-on-the-back meeting at the office."

"Good morning, mom—your child's teacher is calling to share with you how she's not measuring up to others in the class."

"Good morning, business owner—your competition is coming out with something today that's going to leave you playing catch-up."

"Good morning, single friend—look what your social media feed is saying about that girl you went to high school with, the one who got engaged last night. Happy single awareness day (again)."

Another day of longings unfulfilled. That's often what seems to await us.

I recently began understanding this comparison struggle a little too well—not that it suddenly became new to me. It's been there my whole life. But I began to see it as a specific problem that was threatening my day-to-day growth. And after some conversations with others and a lot of time talking to God, He led me to study one comparison-filled Bible story that I have learned so much from. And I've come to a solid conclusion:

Truth will uncover the comparison con.

The Enemy's scam has convinced you and me to believe the lies of being less-than. And maybe it's even seemed like he won. But in this book, I want to give you six truths that, when applied, can help set you up for a comparison comeback. They've helped me find my focus when I've felt like I was falling behind. And I believe they will do the same for you.

We will not let this struggle wreck us. We will learn to love this life again that God has entrusted to us. I will be the best me. You will be the best you. And she will be the best her.

Because truth, like always, will set us free.

And because free women don't need to measure up to anybody. Not even *her*.

With you every step,
Nicki Koziarz

Truth One
You Need to Be Honest

Chapter 1

When Plans Make *Us*

⁓

When You Ask: Why Her?
Truth One: You Need to Be Honest

I AWOKE TO JANUARY MORNING light peering through my bedroom blinds—and to the sense that something wasn't right. A woman knows her body, even a nineteen-year-old girl who's still sort of learning hers. When something's off, you can tell. First you notice, then you wonder why.

Or in my case, you have a sickening feeling you know *exactly* why.

This would explain why I already had a pregnancy test in my purse. This would explain why my first inclination was to sneak quietly into the bathroom and follow the simple directions on the package . . . wait . . . and pray a *help-me-Jesus* prayer.

This would also explain the wave of panic that ran through my body when the double-line indicator that might make one woman squeal with glee and run through the house to show the exciting results to her husband, made me want to . . .

Disappear.

Shock. Disbelief. Fear. Confusion. Chaos.

All of it, in that bathroom with me. A terrifying secret I knew wouldn't stay tucked up in a ball with me there on that floor for very long.

Yet as hard as it is for me to talk about that gut-wrenching morning—even now, these many years later—that day and its aftermath are part of my story. I wrestled with whether to mention it here on these pages or not. I don't like the idea of perhaps inviting unwanted judgment and a critique of me or a discounted opinion of who I am, but . . .

Let's be honest.

Despite being tempted not to share much about my feelings and experiences, I can't think of a better way to set up the struggle that made me want to sit down and write this book to you.

Of all the things that have ever happened to me, the events that spun out from that defining moment in my life ended up spotlighting a secret struggle of mine. It started when I was only a little girl, though it certainly climbed to a much higher level when I became an unwed pregnant woman still in her teens.

This struggle has continued all these years, in ways that still surprise and shock me.

Comparison.
Feeling less-than.
The desire for feeling better-than.
Replacing my reality with my wants.

I have a suspicion you've dealt with or still deal with feelings similar to these. We know it's not good to hold onto these things, but for some reason we still do.

And yet something's just so wrong about all of this. All the misery that comes from looking to the left, looking to the right—ahead, behind—feeling like the unhappiest woman in America. (Now *there's* a title we never hear announced at beauty pageants.)

I've missed so much by holding this posture, missing what is right here to be lived and enjoyed without comparing my past or present or future to somebody else's.

Have you been there too?

Has comparison made you feel like this sometimes?

Then let's go ahead and break out the first of these six truths that are able to start answering the *why her* question in our souls.

Truth One: You Need to Be Honest

Sounds pretty simple, right?

But nothing about our current culture really teaches us to be honest . . . with the possible exception of those ridiculous dressing room mirrors in the department stores—you know, the ones that show three different angles of your backside? Have mercy, too much honesty.

We're good at keeping ourselves away from situations where we're forced to take a long, hard, *honest* look at ourselves. We've learned how to keep a filter wrapped around our souls so that we don't have to see things the way they really are—like how we pick and choose from those filters that help create the flawless pictures we take on our phones.

And you know why?

Comparison.

Comparison is what does this to us. It clouds our sight. It motivates us to create denial. Makes things not look the way they are. But what if we could just be *honest* for a moment? With ourselves? With God? *Honest* about what makes us feel so compelled to compare our lives with others?

You most likely won't be broadcasting your biggest comparison struggles on Facebook tomorrow. But we all have a place—a place that frequently makes us see ourselves as less-than in comparison to someone else. A place where we feel the most intimidated, perhaps a place that goes back to something deeply rooted in our lives. Something rarely shared because we love to shout our successes but seldom show our secret sorrows.

> We love to shout our successes but seldom show our secret sorrows.

But the more honest we can become about these areas that threaten our souls the most, the sooner we'll feel empowered enough to escape this comparison chase. So let's start by being honest right here, starting with the one verse that uncovered this whole struggle in me. Honesty through the filter of God's Word brings an understanding that goes beyond our capacity.

Here it is . . .

In measuring themselves by themselves and comparing themselves to themselves, they lack understanding. (2 Cor. 10:12)

Have you ever had one of those collisions between dreams, plans, and reality that left you a little broken, a little foggy, a little jealous of the world that seemed to be passing you by? I think you probably have. (I know *I* sure have.) We all end up learning at some point, usually the hard way, that sometimes we make our plans, and sometimes we surrender to plans.

Where was that destination you were headed toward before it resulted in a major detour? An invitation you didn't RSVP with a "yes," yet somehow found yourself there anyway?

I can think of many things from my own life: my marriage, my kids, my body, and my career. The fallout from those unhappy seasons can linger a long time. And they can come with an embarrassing mess to clean up.

We don't really want to look at all of that and at what got us there. *Honestly.* You know why? Because these situations would already be bad enough, except they come with the added blow of seeing day after day where things all seem to be working out so well for *her*.

> Sometimes we make our plans, and sometimes we surrender to plans.

Watching *her* live out her hopes and dreams can leave us with an empty gap deep inside. It's always what comes of "measuring" ourselves, "comparing" ourselves, and lacking the "understanding" to just *be* ourselves (2 Cor. 10:12).

God-Struggles

Church ladies know we shouldn't be jealous and envious of *her*. In fact, we know we should actually be happy to see her succeeding. But maybe I'm not such a good church lady because I repeatedly find myself fighting the urge to compare myself with her—this woman who seems to have it all together, all figured out, living a life so full of God's favor. The failure to be honest with others and myself about this struggle has threatened to ruin me. More than once.

Because this isn't just a me-struggle; it's a God-struggle.

Sometimes there are struggles that are just ours. It's who we are. The way we're wired. The way we look, talk, or walk. And there's not always a whole lot you can do about it. But then there are struggles that go against the grain of who God created us to be. They keep us from thriving in our own skin. These are our God-struggles.

> For our struggle is not against flesh and blood, but against the rulers, against the authorities, against the cosmic powers of this darkness, against evil, spiritual forces in the heavens. (Eph. 6:12)

And we can't come out victorious from a God-struggle by clinging to denial and dishonesty.

So let's dismiss denial and dishonesty from our lives and ask honesty to transform our failures and future.

Comparison is a battle to see whose truth—ours or God's—we'll allow to rule our thoughts and actions. We need to let Him reshape our thinking around what's actually true in *her* life (which almost surely isn't as beautiful and blissful as we've built it up to be). But also we need to let Him reshape our thinking around what's actually true in our own lives (which probably isn't as soul-killing as we've let it be).

> Comparison is a battle to see whose truth—ours or God's—we'll allow to rule our thoughts and actions.

There's a way to survive this comparison problem, but only if we'll get God-honest about it. And the best news? He welcomes us to the process.

Trust in him at all times, you people; pour out your hearts before him. God is our refuge. (Ps. 62:8)

Sometimes, though, we're just too close to our own stories to be able to see where the breaks in honesty are happening. We're blinded to the blessings, gifts, and favor of God on our own lives. But here's something I've found to be helpful: find someone who's walked through something even worse than your current reality, and see what you can learn from her story. In doing this, you're not trying to use another's situation as a way of determining how well you're doing, in a *make-yourself-feel-better* type of way. But by shifting your perspective onto someone else's experiences, you can start to see the lies of comparison more clearly, then make the connection to your own life. The real truth they've experienced can open your eyes. *If you'll let it.*

Thankfully, God has put lots of people in His Word for us to learn from because (sorry to say this, but . . .) there are some messed-up people in the Bible! In fact, when it comes to this whole *why her* comparison thing, I'm not sure anybody can top a couple of sisters tucked away in the book of Genesis. Allow me to introduce you to them.

Just Call It Crazy

Rachel and Leah have what I consider one of the hardest comparison stories possible—two sisters who ended up married to the same guy, Jacob.

Most of their story is found in Genesis 29–30. The more you read of their story, the more you want to text about it to your friends with that little monkey emoji, the one holding both hands over its mouth. I don't quite understand everything about this story, and you probably won't either. Some of it is truly shocking.

But if ever a story was able to unpack the *why her* question, it's this one.

Their situation was a little weird—the kind of weird that makes some people wonder how the Bible can ever be relevant to our modern life. I get that. Sometimes the strange cultural dynamics of Bible days are hard to identify with. A lot of things seem so odd and just . . . weird.

But remember, these people lived a really, really, really long time ago, under much different historical conditions. Our modern days would look strange to them too. Like, what if Jesus had a Twitter account? Or tasted the food we eat? *Snickers, Jesus?*

But we have to remember, while their rituals and behaviors may not exactly sound relevant, the Bible is always relevant because it reveals deeply rooted truths that never expire. I'll admit, I'm not always sure how to relate to stories like these from the Bible either. But as far as Rachel and Leah go, I can kind of understand their crazy.

The days immediately after learning I was pregnant were, to say the least, *crazy*. Life fast-forwarded for me at warp speed. I had to grow up quickly and make decisions that felt far beyond my capacity. It wasn't the most ideal setting for discovering how to be comfortable in my own skin.

About six weeks after that morning in the bathroom, I found myself at the altar, saying vows to a man I loved, yet barely knew. Kris and I began to settle into our sweet little third-floor apartment while my stomach began growing to a height and width I didn't know was humanly possible.

Then came the brightest day that my gray soul had seen in a long time, when the doctor said, "It's a girl!" Taylor Marie entered our world with a headful of dirty-blond hair and soft skin that seemed to glow with a heavenly light. I loved her more than my heart could grasp from the moment I held her. But loving someone fiercely isn't always enough to cover life's scars —something we'll soon discover in this story with Rachel and Leah.

Honestly, Taylor was catch-ing us at a challenging time in our young lives, and things wouldn't get any easier anytime soon. Financial struggles, marriage issues, health concerns, the whole shebang . . . with me constantly feeling like *that*

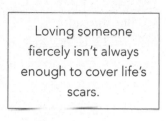

> Loving someone fiercely isn't always enough to cover life's scars.

girl, you know, the one who got pregnant before she was mar-ried. I constantly thought people were thinking things like, "Nice couple, those two, but you know they *had* to get married."

Still, somehow we've made it.

We've tackled the odds. I'm now a wife of seventeen years, with three girls—Taylor, Hope, and Kennedy. They're beautiful and lovable, yes. But three daughters also bring a whole level of insanity one could never predict.

And because we apparently needed even *more* crazy in our lives, we decided to move our family out to a little piece of land we've affectionately nicknamed "The Fixer-Upper Farm." It totally lives up to its name because of all the broken things, lots and lots of broken things. And the smells. Oh mercy, the smells—especially with a barnyard full of misfit animals, including my favorite: the donkeys. (You'll hear more about them later.)

In the South we have this saying: *We don't hide crazy. We put it on our front porch with a glass of sweet tea.* It's hysterically true. And I wholeheartedly admit the Fixer-Upper Farm is its own brand of crazy. I mean, our pug thinks he's a farm dog. Far from it, but we let him sit on the front porch and pretend.

I know you have a lot of crazy too. And we may not be apples-to-apples with each other or with Rachel and Leah, but we've all got our wild issues we deal with.

But through this Bible story filled with lying and deception and manipulation and competition—and even polygamy—it's crazy upon crazy. And if God can use their weird, messy, and complicated lives to teach us wisdom, what could God do through our own honesty with this struggle?

Compromised Plans

Since we're being completely honest here, I could tell you some other things about myself, beyond the getting pregnant at nineteen part. I could open my heart enough to tell you about the comparison struggles that have turned into many hidden hurdles I've had to get over. Things like how I can sometimes become jealous of people, how I can easily feel threatened about the level of my abilities, or how I can be oversensitive to signals that indicate to me I'm being pushed aside.

I could also tell you about another little unknown fact I've hidden behind for years. Despite how insignificant it may seem to you when you hear it, it's been a major source of my comparison issues. So here I go . . .

I never finished college.

Maybe you were hoping for more of a Lifetime movie-worthy type of confession? But I wish you knew all the lies that have built up in my head over time surrounding this one big disappointment. It's convinced me of my unworthiness as a person. It's suffocated my social sanity and my trust in my own potential. I've allowed it to define me for a long, long time.

In the midst of enjoying my senior year of high school, I thought I was all set to go to the finest college my GPA would allow. Which, let's be honest, I knew would be slim picking since I'd let my social life take priority over my academic life.

I was sure, once I got settled into said college, I'd find my Prince Charming, we'd marry, and he would whisk me off into the sunset. We'd adopt at least three kids from Africa. *Probably start our own orphanage.* We would always laugh. Our house would be encircled by a perfectly white picket fence, dotted with the most beautiful, colorful rose bushes. And he would constantly tell me how beautiful I was, every single day.

I'll wait while you gag. But that's not far from how naïve and unrealistic my thinking was at the time. (If you could only see the disease-stricken rose bushes I have now. #blackthumb.) So you can only imagine my tears and confusion when I stood in my parents' kitchen one day, holding my college rejection letter.

What?! No! This was my dream. This was supposed to be my next destination. There was no other plan. This was it.

And yet here, with the opening of one thin white envelope, all of it was gone. The only option left to me now was community college. I couldn't believe my college-of-choice dream was gone, and many days of crying followed.

Never had my younger self experienced this level of depression and unhappiness before—especially as I helped my friends buy new bedding for their dorm rooms, attended their farewell parties, watched them drive away to their exciting new adventures—while I stayed behind, alone, wondering why *they* were getting to live out the reality I'd been planning all along for *me*.

Going to college is what kids in our culture do, right? We finish high school; we go to college. (Not a hundred percent true, but . . .) As far as I was concerned, the college I wanted to go to was *everything*.

Only a few months later I would find myself in that bathroom, holding that pregnancy test. And with *that* on top of it, the more I looked at others, the less value I saw in myself. Disappointment led to one compromising decision after another. I chased the things I thought would fill that void of disappointment. Comparison convinces us to chase the many things we can when we can't have the one thing we want.

> Comparison convinces us to chase the many things we can when we can't have the one thing we want.

All this chasing ultimately led me to feeling like one giant disappointment. To my parents, church leaders, friends, and to *myself.* When anything other than God becomes our everything, disappointment is soon to follow.

What's Your Everything?

Let's take it back about four thousand years, where in Rachel and Leah's world *babies* were everything. Having babies during this time encompassed so much of a woman's identity. And throughout this two-sister story, as we'll repeatedly see, the issue of having children (and not being able to have children) became a key point of comparison between them.

The struggle with infertility had begun a generation earlier. Their husband Jacob's parents, Isaac and Rebekah, experienced at least some level of struggle in the getting-pregnant department. We know this because the Bible tells us that "Isaac prayed to the LORD on behalf of his wife because she was childless" (Gen. 25:21).

So this might be another good place for being honest.

I realize I may be bringing up a subject that's tender for someone. And I can't totally relate. But just because someone's struggle isn't the same as mine doesn't mean I shouldn't seek to understand. I know there are women reading these pages who are married, single, divorced, or widowed, some who are dealing with empty hearts in this particular life-plan area.

Just as I still cringe a bit whenever someone asks me where I went to college or what my degree is in, this could be a comparison point—when you hear other women's pregnancy announcements or see moms with babies at the grocery store.

Or maybe its something else altogether, coming from some other tender soul place.

But we all have a place.

And we all need to be honest about it.

Honesty is what gives us the chance to become hopeful that we can overcome this struggle. Becoming transparent about what causes us to compare ourselves to others the most will keep us from needing to compare ourselves to others at all.

Otherwise, we'll keep heading down this path toward comparison destruction.

Fueled by discontentment and discouragement, we'll get into the toxic habit of looking, and staring, then looking again. We'll keep wondering what's so wrong with us, questioning our worth, and even doubting God.

Then as *she* seems to walk off with our happy, we'll secretly whisper, "Why her?" to the all–too-receptive audience we find in our own hearts. And every time we ask the question, it will trail off, unanswered . . . because there *is* no answer.

Unless we're willing to live with *honest* answers.

~ This & That ~

Wrestle with this:

What is something comparison has convinced you to chase?

Remember that:

We love to shout our successes but seldom show our secret sorrows.

Comparison is a battle to see whose truth—ours or God's—we'll allow to rule our thoughts and actions.

Comparison convinces us to chase the many things we can when we can't have the one thing we want.

Chapter 2

Honest Answers

~~

When You Ask: Why Her?
Truth One: You Need to Be Honest

I DON'T HAVE A SISTER. But I do have three daughters. And I'm not sure there's anything quite like sister honesty.

My girls are quick to point out each other's flaws. I don't think they do it to be mean-spirited toward each other. They just feel the freedom to say what they want to say. If someone arrives at the dinner table with a fresh pimple on her face? It will definitely get a mention. If someone's outfit is a fashion fail? There will be no consideration of hurt feelings. If someone's hair needs to be washed? Or her breath is funky? There's no such thing as a safe-flawed-zone in a house full of girls. Whether you ask a question or not, honesty is coming.

And it starts at such a young age.

You know how people will come up and just randomly tell your kids how cute they are? My oldest, Taylor, got so used to it that after her sister Hope Ann was born, she would get insulted if others gawked over Hope. Once I was with both of the girls at Walmart and a sweet elderly lady came up to our buggy. She smiled and said, "I don't know which one is prettier, this one or that one." Taylor pointed at herself and firmly shouted, "THIS ONE." I still smile whenever I think about two-year-old, confidently beautiful Taylor.

I never had to teach my girls to compare their physical appearances. They figured it out on their own. And still every day we look at someone else and find a reason for not liking something about ourselves.

It's a timeless struggle.

Just ask Leah.

Isn't That Nice?

In the first chapter, we briefly met Jacob's parents and learned about their infertility struggle. Isaac prayed for his wife, Rebekah, to bear children, and the Lord answered with a double blessing— twin boys, Esau and Jacob.

Their sibling rivalry started with battling each other inside the womb (Gen. 25:22, 26), followed by Esau trading his birthright for a pot of stew (Gen. 25:27–33). *Men take their food so seriously.*

Also, Jacob tricked their elderly, half-blind father into giving him the firstborn blessing (Gen. 27:1–40). Things got so bad between the two of them that Esau swore that the minute their father was dead, he would make sure his twin brother wasn't far behind.

To keep these two from killing each other, Rebekah and Isaac decided they needed to send Jacob out of harm's way.

Isaac called Jacob and blessed him and directed him, "You must not take a wife from the Canaanite women. Arise,

go to Paddan-aram to the house of Bethuel your mother's
father, and take as your wife from there one of the daughters of Laban your mother's brother." (Gen. 28:1–2 ESV)

That's how Jacob ended up at the community well in a far-off
village, where he struck up a conversation with some of the locals
asking if they knew of a man named Laban. *Know* him? *Of course*
they knew him. Not only did they know him, but look, "Here is
his daughter Rachel, coming with his sheep" (Gen. 29:6).

Love began at that well.

When Rachel smiled, and Jacob was smitten.

She made an immediate impression on Jacob. No sooner
had he introduced himself and made the family connection than
he kissed her (v. 11)! *Fast moves, Jacob.* Rachel ran off to tell her
father about it, and Jacob and Laban shook hands on a deal: Jacob
offered to work seven years for the hand of Rachel in marriage.

Now depending on how much of a romantic you are, the
thought of this deal will either make you gag or give a big love
sigh. I mean, how stinkin' sweet is it that Jacob was willing to
work seven years for this woman? Seriously. But to add a note
of dramatic conflict to the story, there was soon to be another
woman involved, Laban's *other* daughter, Rachel's older sister,
Leah—although the Bible is not very kind in how it describes her.

Leah's eyes were weak, but Rachel was beautiful in form
and appearance. (Gen. 29:17 ESV)

All kinds of opinions exist about the meaning of this description concerning her "weak" eyes, but you can boil them all down
to this: Rachel was beautiful; Leah was not. The first form of comparison we see in this story is based on appearance.

And of all places . . . IN THE BIBLE. Our physical appearances may be up for critique, but at least we are not being compared with each other in the Bible!

Wonder what it was like for Leah growing up in the shadow of her beautiful kid sister? I'm sure this wasn't the first time comparison had raised its ugly head in their relationship. I'm guessing she'd been made to feel less-than on many different occasions.

So when Rachel showed up at the house with the man she was going to marry, I wouldn't be surprised if Leah experienced a little bit of what you might call the "must be nice" syndrome.

Maybe you've had a symptom or two show up from that syndrome. *Me too, friend.*

Recently I was sitting in a meeting where someone brought up the new house that one of our mutual friends had just moved into. It really is *quite* the spread. Everything is brand spanking new, huge kitchen with a butler's pantry, and with all the perfect touches of light fixtures and furnishings.

My mind immediately drifted into comparison mode, thinking of our Fixer-Upper Farm which, while beautiful to me, is definitely what its nickname implies: a true fixer-upper. And you've got to have patience with a fixer-upper—something comparison loves to make me forget.

I turned to the coworker sitting nearest me (who was probably thinking the same thing about her own house), and we said almost in unison, "Must be nice, huh?"

Must be nice.
Good for her.
Wow.
I wish I had . . .

These thoughts are such subtle forms of comparison.

So I can imagine Leah sitting there watching this Jacob thing play out with her sister, and maybe some subtle thoughts slipped in . . .

Must be nice Rachel has someone interested in her.

Must be nice everyone considers her the pretty one.

Must be nice our daddy thinks she's worth seven years of work.

These "must be nice" thoughts can slip in anywhere, can't they? They're really at the core of our comparison struggle. We don't even need a sister like Rachel to plant the seed. I bet you can think of a time right now, back when you were a little girl, when your first *must be nice* thought slipped in.

I remember mine.

Saddle Shoes

I spent the first few years of my childhood in the small town of Coolidge, Arizona, about halfway between Phoenix and Tucson. My family was by no means well-off. We always seemed to have just enough to get by. Rarely was there room in our budget for extras, like the pair of black-and-white saddle shoes I desperately wanted. Do you remember those? They were calling my name in 1985.

My dad was the high school football coach, so I spent a lot of Friday nights with my mom and brother in the bleachers. The game itself was anything but thrilling to me, but I didn't mind going because it meant I'd be able to watch the cheerleaders. *That* was exciting!

I dreamed of the day when I, too, might hopefully be out there in a pleated skirt with pom-poms, making the crowd roar with enthusiasm for our team. The cheerleaders must have known how much I looked up to them because in the middle of one football season, they invited my best friend and me to come cheer with them at an upcoming game.

Our elementary schoolgirl excitement was out of control. High school cheerleaders?! YES! We practiced in the backyard every chance we could get leading up to the game. One afternoon, we even put on our homemade uniforms.

But my zeal for this opportunity quickly faded that day as I looked down at my friend's feet. She was wearing a pair of brand new, shiny, black-and-white saddle shoes. The same kind the high school cheerleaders wore. My thoughts screamed silently with envy: *What? Where did she get those? I need a pair too!*

I went to my mom later that night and pleaded for saddle shoes, knowing full well our bank account didn't match my begging. No matter what I said, it didn't matter. We didn't have the money.

Must be nice, though, being a girl in a family who did.

But this event in my life, especially as I look back on it, helped me discover something about comparison that stuck with me. Honesty teaches us to stop fearing what we don't have so we can see what we do.

> Honesty teaches us to stop fearing what we don't have so we can see what we do.

Right before that big football game, my mom actually did find a pair of black-and-white saddle shoes I could borrow from someone else. No, they weren't shiny and new like my friend's were. In fact, they were pretty scuffed up and a little tight on my feet. But even though they were obviously not as nice—not as *beautiful*, to use Rachel and Leah's comparison word—I was thrilled with them. I took pride in them. I loved them.

I mean, sure, every time I looked at my BFF in her saddle shoes, I felt a little stab of jealousy and discontent. But there were no new saddle shoes coming to me. I knew that. And by accepting the shoes I had, I was able to get *honest* with myself about it. To be okay with it. I decided I didn't want my envy to ruin the excitement of this opportunity.

Honesty about the source of our comparison issues can lead us toward being hopeful again. Admitting the situations we face each day that try to make us feel less-than is an important first step—recognizing them as soon as possible, calling them out before they take root and spiral into a lifestyle. Being honest enough to call out comparison the moment it happens will help us regain our control of it.

Maybe you don't desire to be the number-one person in your company. Maybe you don't care if your house looks anything like a Pinterest picture. Maybe things like college educations don't really faze you. But *something does.* Some sour reality that makes you feel like you're not measuring up. And until you get honest about it, you won't be able to conquer it.

For Leah, it was this situation with Rachel and Jacob—the latest blow in a lifelong comparison struggle with her sister. For you, it's yours. For me, it's mine. And when I think about these struggles in my own life, and what it means to be honest about them, God often takes me back to this verse:

Each one should test their own actions. Then they can take pride in themselves alone, without comparing themselves to somebody else. (Gal. 6:4 NIV)

Comparison can sneak into my heart no matter how strong my level of gratefulness and awareness. But by taking the time to recognize and thank God for the blessings He puts into my life each day—by taking a good, holy, healthy kind of pride in my current situation—I'm much more able to stay honest and content with who I am and who I'm not. Staring too long at the success of someone else can make us miss our own satisfaction with life.

And there's simply too much that's beautiful about *you* and *me* to lose it all on *her.*

Desperate Moments

When I think back on that season after I discovered I was pregnant, *desperation* is the most accurate way to describe it. Desperate to be around people who would still accept me. Desperate about my life plans that were changing quickly. Desperate to understand how I'd found myself in this position at such a young age. And the next few years of my life, if I'm being honest, were filled with even *more* desperation, which led to decisions that were often destructive.

That's because desperation, I've found, is deceptive. It convinces us we're immune from the chain reaction our choices bring. It leads us to confuse what we want with what we think we deserve. When life is less than we expected, we often make desperate, destructive decisions.

What would you tell the younger version of yourself? There are so many things I wish I could tell the younger version of *my*self. Things like, be patient. Stay close to God. Be you. Believe the best about others.

But really, these things are not that much different from what I'd tell this *current* version of myself. Dissatisfaction still tries to distract me. Feeling less-than when I'm around other people and other kids' parents and the cute women at work can still lure me toward the desperation of not measuring up. But . . . honesty teaches us to walk through desperate moments without having to do destructive things.

> Honesty teaches us to walk through desperate moments without having to do destructive things.

Leah is about to find herself in a desperate situation. Let's see what we can learn from how she handles it.

The seven years were up. The day had finally come. Jacob had "worked seven years for Rachel, and they seemed like only a few days to him because of his love for her" (Gen. 29:20). But what happened next was just pure awful. Somehow, under cover of darkness, within the mysterious wedding customs of this ancient society, Laban was able to pull off a shameful trick. On *everybody*.

> That evening, Laban took his daughter Leah and gave her to Jacob, and he slept with her. . . . When morning came, there was Leah! So he said to Laban, "What is this you have done to me? Wasn't it for Rachel that I worked for you? Why have you deceived me?" (Gen. 29:23, 25)

If this had taken place today, I'd say Leah's therapy bill would be out of control. Can you imagine your own dad using you to trick someone like *that*? It was bad enough that she lived in her sister's shadow her entire life, but to be tossed into a situation sure to make things even worse? It's just awful.

Before she knew it, she was married to a man who didn't love her. And a week later, after Laban had swindled Jacob into committing to seven *more* years of work, her sister Rachel joined the family as Jacob's other wife. His preferred wife. His beloved, beautiful wife.

Can you say "Unhappily Ever After?"

That's the title of the story I thought *my* life was writing after watching my college dream fade into the background, after becoming pregnant, even after marrying into an unknown, unexpected future. It hardly set the stage for a best-selling fairy tale.

I tried covering up the hurt—like we do, whether it's with food, debt, shopping, escapes, addictions, habits, or behaviors. By God's grace, I functioned when I thought it was impossible. But I was miserable. Broken. Desperate. I lost touch with who I was, trying to become someone I wasn't. We often lose who we are while trying to become someone we aren't.

> We often lose who we are while trying to become someone we aren't.

My three girls came along, one by one. Our marriage settled into a rhythm. I loved my husband deeply, and our daughters became such a great delight in my life. And yet, when the girls were napping or asleep at night, the unsettling of my soul would surface.

Secret questions fumbled through my thoughts, and I became consumed with everything I didn't have and how I didn't measure up. That's when I really started thinking more often about *her*. "Why her?" I felt like the circumstances of my life were challenging enough that I could ask it. But in reality, it was more than my circumstances.

My soul was sick. The combination of trying days and a troubled soul became the perfect emotional storm, stealing my joy, life, trust, and meaning . . . most important, stealing my hope.

I wondered some days if I would ever be happy again.

"Unhappily Ever After" can title any of our lives. Maybe it's where you are today. Its roots may be freshly planted, or they may be so deep they've been there for what seems like a lifetime. But it doesn't have to stay. God has given us a longing to know Him and be known by Him. And when we're honest with Him, He can cause things to happen—both in our hearts as well as in our circumstances—that can lead us out of comparison toward freedom and restoration.

Be Wiser

There's a lot we don't know about what this unhappy season was like for Leah, though I think we can all agree her life had gone from bad to worse. But if you read between the lines, you can spot some honesty happening. As I've studied her story, here's what I *don't* see.

> *I don't see her throwing a fit.*
>
> *I don't see her begging for things to be different.*
>
> *I don't see her throwing herself on Jacob to try winning him over.*

31

This doesn't mean her heart wasn't aching, her eyes weren't leaking, and her soul wasn't still asking, "Why her?" In fact, we'll see Leah wander away from this quiet place as the story of her life unfolds.

But for now, maybe (we don't know for sure) she was just trying to be honest. She knew how she'd gotten here. She knew what she was up against. She knew the differences between herself and her beautiful sister. And instead of going insane over this struggle, maybe she knew enough not to keep comparing. Just to try being herself.

To stay quiet instead of competitive.

> Honesty can lead us to quiet places where we seek to understand rather than merely react.

Honesty can lead us to quiet places where we seek to understand rather than merely react. We don't become doormats for the world to wipe its unfair feet on, but we are able to walk into those places where we've felt the urge to compare ourselves to others. And amazingly, we find something else waiting for us there. When we choose honesty over comparison, we gain wisdom.

For the Lord gives wisdom; from his mouth come knowledge and understanding. (Prov. 2:6)

Through God's grace and mercy working through our honesty, we're able to tap into an ability that helps us see past our insecurities and embrace a deeper level of maturity and perspective.

Webster's *Learner's Dictionary* defines wisdom as: "the natural ability to understand things that most other people cannot understand." I love that! Wisdom helps us move beyond the question,

"Why is this happening?" to ask a wiser question: "What can I do about it?"

When I feel like a failure, when life seems incredibly unfair, when everyone else seems to be getting further ahead and I'm falling apart, I don't need any more information to help me know what to do. We've got more than enough information, advice, and input at our fingertips. But I desperately need God's wisdom to help me see what I can or can't control, help me see what I can or can't change, and help me be honest enough to say, "Yes, girl, here's an area where I'm struggling with comparison, and I need to admit it and call it out."

> Wisdom helps us move beyond the question, "Why is this happening?" to ask a wiser question: "What can I do about it?"

Wisdom isn't something God forces on us; it's something He gives us to focus on.

God does that when we're honest with Him.

He knows what we need and so freely gives it to us.

Could anything be more comforting than what He did for Leah when He saw her struggling and hurting as an unwanted wife, while her sister was being welcomed with seven years' worth of desire?

> When the LORD saw that Leah was unloved, he opened her womb; but Rachel was unable to conceive. (Gen. 29:31)

That's how much God loves us. When we find ourselves in situations that appear to be ruining us, He will give us the grace to survive what comparison can do to us. Choosing honesty with

God will give us understanding and a powerful perspective to look beyond what we can see. Ultimately, the honesty we find in trusting His gift of wisdom brings us hope.

Honest Answers

As we wrap up this first truth to our *why her* struggle, we need to look around our own lives for a minute. I know there's a lot of "Unhappily Ever After" we could focus on if we wanted. Like Leah, we may not need to look far to see what others are doing and getting and enjoying that makes them so happy.

The practical side of our brains thinks we know the answers to this *why her* question. Answers like: She's prettier. She's smarter. She's thinner. She's more talented than we are. We recognize the patterns, the behaviors, the habits that seem to guarantee *her* success.

But even as we're looking, we're missing it.

Because that's not honesty.

First, if we're honest, we'll realize some parts of our own stories are still being written. And if we rush to cover up those pieces of our lives that lend themselves the most to comparison, we'll miss the powerful story of redemption that God is in the middle of writing.

We've yet to see His work in some of our comparison struggles, but I'll share this: God has helped me live with a new mindset on those parts that I've become honest about and wrestled through.

And the rest of the parts? I know those will come around in time as I keep approaching them with honesty and applying His wisdom.

Second, this uniquely beautiful, unexplainable life that God is building in each of us was never meant to look exactly like someone else's, regardless of the message our culture shouts at us. It tries to tell us what's good, lovely, and dreamy. Culture tells us to set our eyes on *IT*—this impossible standard, this prize that none of us can quite identify. But while we cannot control how the world tries to classify us, we *can* control what we chase.

Honesty about those places where we feel the need to compare will set us free from what we think we've lost or missed or wasted too much time considering. Honesty

> While we cannot control how the world tries to classify us, we *can* control what we chase.

will help us move forward and find answers that can counteract the damage this *why her* question has done to our souls.

So in light of this first truth—Truth One: "You need to be honest"—I'm going to ask you to become incredibly honest with yourself. Using the prompts below, have an honest conversation with yourself and God. You can do this here in this book or in your journal.

- First, list any areas where you're sensing a "must be nice" syndrome slipping in.
- Second, describe any part of your life right now that feels like an "Unhappily Ever After" situation.
- Third, write five things you're grateful for.
- And fourth, write a prayer to God, asking Him to help you stay honest and aware of this comparison struggle.

∼ This & That ∼

Wrestle with this:

Who was someone you compared yourself to as a child?

Remember that:

Honesty teaches us to stop fearing what we don't have so we can see what we do.

We often lose who we are while trying to become someone we aren't.

Honesty can lead us to quiet places where we seek to understand rather than merely react.

Truth Two
See It Like It Really Is

Chapter 3

Maybe Now

———

When You Ask: Why Her?
Truth Two: See It Like It Really Is

THERE'S THE STORY WE SEE, and then there's the story of what's really happening.

We live in a culture where photographing a moment is on our agenda almost every day. I recently read an article that said the world captures about 1.2 trillion pictures in a year. *What?!* That is a LOT of pictures—of our food, our pets, our families, but especially of our moments. I mean, if there's not a picture of it, did it really happen? And even if it did, did it really happen like that?

Life looks beautiful across our social media platforms. It seems like we've got this thing together and our lives are just full of happy, blissful moments. But it's not always like it seems, is it?

A few summers ago, our family vacationed at one of our favorite beach spots for a few days. It was a great trip, with lots of fun pictures posted on Instagram.

With the exception of the last day.

When things got very non-picture worthy.

My youngest daughter, Kennedy, was in a fierce mood after too many nights of staying up way too late, too much junk food,

too much sun, and too much time together. Just as we were pack-
ing up to leave, she got a tiny splinter in her foot. One thing to
note about my Kennedy: she has z-e-r-o tolerance for pain. I knew
this was going to be *super fun* trying to get this thing out.

And so began the screams, the tears, and the horrible things
kids say to you when you're trying to do something that will actually help them. I was positive someone was about to call Child
Protective Services because I'm sure her screams of "DO NOT
TOUCH ME!" and "GET YOUR HANDS OFF ME!" could be
heard all the way to the ocean shore.

Frustrated, I said some unkind things and threatened to take
her and her splinter to the ER if she didn't stop screaming. But
my threats only made her scream louder. And louder. And louder.
Nothing I could do or say would make her calm down. Not until
after the longest two hours—yes, two hours!—of my life did I
finally get the splinter out.

The silence was a relief when it came, but I was a mess, and
so was Kennedy. I was embarrassed and crying for how I yelled at
her. She was embarrassed and crying because she had been so dramatic. And my husband and other two daughters were mad that
the last few hours of our trip had been spent like this.

No one was speaking, just throwing things in the car.

How lovely. Yes, let's take a picture of this.

Since that part didn't make it onto my Instagram story, anyone
looking through our vacation pictures would assume the entire
thing was so perfect. But things are not always as they appear. Not
just in *your* life. Not just in *my* life. But also in *her* life. This fear of
ours, the one that says our life and our experience isn't normal (or
isn't right, or isn't okay)—just because it's not perfect, just because
it's not like *hers*—is a lie.

I have so many issues with that word *normal*—because it's nothing other than a comparison word. It's a measurement of my life compared to yours. And almost always, what I think about *your* life (and what you think about *my* life) is not entirely based in reality. So we need to remember, when looking at people's lives that appear perfect to us, there's probably a not-so-perfect story happening there that's never going to be told. Because we've all got our ugly. For most of us, it's just more hidden than our beautiful.

> We need to remember, when looking at people's lives that appear perfect to us, there's probably a not-so-perfect story happening there that's never going to be told.

This is why we need *honesty* (Truth One). And yet honesty will only take us part of the way. Honesty helps us become more aware of what's going on in our own hearts and in our own circumstances. But to take us to the next step, where we become more in tune with the world that exists all around us, we need a second truth.

Truth Two: See It Like It Really Is

Two important things to mention about this truth and what it takes to see through the deception.

First, *it takes work*. Depending on where you look, within all the information and updates and news about world happenings that bombard you every day, you'll find exactly what you hope to discover.

For instance, how many times have you thought you heard someone say something on social media, only to go back and discover it was someone else? Or how many articles have you read that created a sense of fear or panic, only to look a little closer and realize it was a false source of information or from ten years ago? Ever had this happen? Me too.

We scroll so quickly through our phones that it's hard to remember who said what, when, and where. We lose perspective on what's really happening. One day, if it hasn't already, all this virtual connectedness is going to catch up with us.

In my experience, both personally and in journeying with other people, I've learned that when God needs us to see something really important about ourselves and the world around us, it takes the hard work of uncovering, because our Enemy is working desperately to cover it up. Daily we need to whisper this prayer:

> God, give me eyes to see what I need to see,
> not what I want to see.

So yes, this takes work. It takes intentional efforts each day.

Second, *it takes light*. Ephesians 5:13 says, "When anything is exposed by the light, it becomes visible" (ESV). This verse is one of many in Scripture that speaks to the importance of staying in the light. It means building our lives on what God's Word and His Spirit illuminate for us, rather than stumbling around in the chaos and confusion of the darkness.

God doesn't expose us to His light to shame us, guilt-trip us, or make us feel less than someone else. He exposes us to light because He doesn't want us to become drowned by deception (see 1 John 4:1). He wants us to see what's really happening in front of us.

I learned this truth again recently. The work I've been doing in crafting the words of this book has meant a lot of sitting, which isn't the best position for your body. So to help deal with some of the aches and stiffness, I purchased one of those giant foam rollers to help me stretch out my back each night.

Whenever I'm done with it, I try to remember to put it away in the closet, but the other night I accidently left it out. Somehow, though, it ended up rolling in front of our bathroom door. Where it sat, black and unseen, until Kris, my husband, got up to go to the bathroom and found it with one of his bare feet. Which then had a nicely swollen toe to go along with it.

That's what happens when we walk in the dark. We can so easily become oblivious to what's happening around us, blinded to how things really are. And if we're not careful, one of the things we'll start tripping over is the trap of comparison. *Softly. Subtly. Quietly.* We need to courageously ask God to open our eyes, to keep us in the light, especially when we're entertaining a *why her* thought.

That simple prayer seems to be exactly what I need over and over again.

> God, give me eyes to see what I need to see,
> not what I want to see.

Otherwise, we'll fall for the deception of comparison.
Like two long-ago sisters I could name.

Maybe Now

The last we saw of Rachel and Leah in the previous chapter, Laban had tricked Jacob into taking Leah as his wife—seven years of work for a woman he didn't even want. It was a messy little scenario all the way around—for Jacob, of course, but especially for Leah. And yet we're about to see God's compassion for her.

> When the LORD saw that Leah was unloved, he opened her womb; but Rachel was unable to conceive. (Gen. 29:31)

I believe, as I mentioned in the last chapter, Leah started out dealing with this comparison issue with as much honesty as she could muster. We know her unloved heart attracted God's compassionate attention. He stepped in to show Leah that He was with her, that He saw her, and that He was going to bless her despite Jacob's lack of love for her.

I love that.

But there's something else in this story we need to look at a little closer. Something we need to see like it really is. As you read the following verse, pay close attention to the last few words.

> Leah conceived, gave birth to a son, and named him Reuben, for she said, "The LORD has seen my affliction; surely my husband will love me now." (Gen. 29:32)

God had blessed Leah in the midst of her burden. But sometimes, like Leah, we want His blessing to mean what *we* want it to mean. We want to see it the way *we* want to see it. God, however, sees the bigger picture and knows what will bless us most in light of the story He is writing.

The words we hear Leah saying in this verse (and in other verses that follow) should raise a flag of caution. "Surely my husband will love me now." That single word—*surely*—contains so much confidence and presumption in it.

Leah looked at the blessing God had given her in her firstborn son, and she saw it as a tool for manipulating a bad situation, for causing her husband to notice her, pay attention to her, and see something special in her. She saw it as a weapon to launch into the middle of her comparison battle with her sister so that she could get Jacob's heart, the one thing Rachel had that Leah wanted most. However, God's blessings are never meant to be a redemption bullet we shoot into someone else's life.

God didn't bless Leah to burden Jacob or Rachel. God didn't bless Leah to prove she was more valuable than Rachel. God blessed Leah to help her know she was loved by Him and to bring glory to Himself by fulfilling His purposes through her life.

> Whenever we view His blessings as a way of gaining others' respect or of putting ourselves ahead of a perceived rival, we're counteracting what God is trying to do in us.

Whenever we view His blessings as a way of gaining others' respect or of putting ourselves ahead of a perceived rival, we're counteracting what God is trying to do in us. We're not seeing things the way they really are.

Unfortunately, Leah's misreading of what was happening to her was only the beginning.

She conceived again, gave birth to a son, and said, "The LORD heard that I am unloved and has given me this son also." So she named him Simeon.

She conceived again, gave birth to a son, and said, "At last, my husband will become attached to me because

I have borne three sons for him." Therefore he was named Levi. (Gen. 29:33–34)

See the progression? Or rather the *lack* of progression? The rut? See how these thoughts, these desires, these words—this turning of blessings into redemption bullets—only emptied her heart even more?

Baby One: *Maybe now* Jacob will love me.

Baby Two: *Maybe now* Jacob will love me.

Baby Three: *Maybe now* Jacob will love me.

All those babies, and still no love for Leah.

She'd turned this into a competition for Jacob's heart. But we're not in competition with other people. We receive God's blessings for what *He* intends, to make us who *we* are and should be, not to get what other people have or to keep up with what other people do.

Climbing Charts

First jobs are filled with so much anticipation and excitement. My first job was as a cashier at a local grocery store. And I loved it. My childhood days of playing grocery store paid off! Literally.

I loved the interaction with people, loved the beeping noise the scanner made as you slid the groceries across it. And I loved making conversation as I worked.

Then one afternoon I noticed a chart someone had posted in the break room—a tally of how many minutes it took each cashier to scan a certain number of grocery items. The ones at the top of the list had stars and smiles next to their names, visual evidence of their success. But my name wasn't up at the top. My name, I quickly found, was at the bottom.

And immediately, comparison began to convince me I needed to catch up.

So I started paying close attention to the faster cashiers' skill sets, to see how they were able to work so much more quickly and effectively than I did. The biggest thing I noticed was how few moments they spent talking to the customers. Their primary focus was on getting people through their lines as quickly as possible.

So I started to follow suit with their actions. I changed to become what I thought was expected of me. And at first it worked. My name slowly but surely moved up on that list.

And yet my items-scanned-per-minute ratio wasn't the only thing that was changing. I was also starting to hate my job. Comparison had turned into competitiveness in me.

And one day, my catch-up competitive plan backfired on me.

A woman came through my line with a number of grocery items, at the end of which was a birthday cake. She was obviously very frazzled—and made certain I *knew* she was frazzled. From her party planning, I assumed. But I was in a hurry, too, because, *hello!*—cashier competition.

In my rush to get her quickly through the checkout, I didn't see some of the other items that were behind the birthday cake. And as I kept the conveyor belt rolling, they began to press up against the cake. By the time I saw what was happening, it was too late. The cake was smushed.

And, oh, did this smushing of her cake send her already frazzled self into a frenzy of madness. She yelled—*screamed*, actually—while I apologized over and over. Then taking one look at my name tag, she barked out some words I'll never forget. "Let me tell you something, Miss, uh . . . 'NICKI.' My day is about to get better. But your day? It's about to get worse!"

She snatched the receipt out of my hands and stomped off into the manager's office, where she told him exactly why I should be fired on the spot. Overreacting a bit? Yes, I think so. But I still felt horrible that I had ruined this woman's cake.

I had lost sight of what made my job enjoyable. I had become somebody I wasn't made to be, and had actually become less capable as an employee rather than better—all because of that ridiculous cashier comparison chart in the break room.

But I wanted acceptance. I wanted validation. I didn't want my name to be on the bottom of that list. And in trying to change it, in chasing those desires, my view of reality slipped out of focus. I had become miserable while trying to keep up with other people. I was no longer seeing things the way they really were.

So I can identify with the heart behind Leah's *maybe now* struggle. Comparison brings out our competitive streak, which eats away at our contentment, which then starts to destroy our confidence, until we're fighting to keep up with an unrealistic standard.

> Comparison brings out our competitive streak, which eats away at our contentment, which then starts to destroy our confidence, until we're fighting to keep up with an unrealistic standard.

Maybe now that I have these shoes, I'll feel pretty.

Maybe now that I have this couch, I'll have friends over.

Maybe now that this person is talking to me, this thing I want will happen.

Maybe now that I've got this job, things will really take off for me.

Maybe now makes it all about *me* being better than *her*. It tries to convince me that just one more step, one more thing, one more relationship, one more promotion, will be the key that leads to long-term contentment, in comparison with *her*.

But I've discovered something important in the process. The *desire* part is not really the problem. Desiring things isn't bad, unless our desires become greater than the One who gives desires.

For instance, Leah's desire to have children was not wrong. Over the years I've had desires for things, for relationships, for finances, for all kinds of stuff that are not bad to want. Desiring them isn't what's destructive. They become destructive when the desire becomes an idol, something that feeds our selfish desire to compete and compare.

> Desiring things isn't bad, unless our desires become greater than the One who gives desires.

Maybe now is such a perception deception. It's fueled by a world that continually affirms our lack of measuring up to the woman next to us, across from us, or in our newsfeed. It tells us there's always more to strive toward. It plays games with our confidence—confidence which we must always keep in control, because too much of it, or too little of it, can mess with a woman's soul. If we're not careful, we'll be living with a *maybe now* mentality for the rest of our lives, leading us to more and more disappointment.

This Time

I know this whole sister-wives thing between Rachel and Leah is kind of crazy and not normal for the culture we live in now. But in our society today, if you do something out of what's considered "normal," they'll probably put you on TV.

Occasionally I've peeked at a reality show based on a family that lives the polygamist lifestyle, out of sheer curiosity with questions like, *"How are they not jealous all the time?"* In my peeking, I've never found the answer to those questions. But I personally could never feel valued enough knowing my husband loved another woman. I would constantly be in a state of insecurity, fear, and jealousy.

Leah certainly felt that. She was having babies, and that was good. Being a mother gave her something positive in her life. But she remained in a situation where her husband didn't love her. And at the core of Leah's soul, all she wanted was to be loved. It influenced her toward this *maybe now* journey, which she battled for years through three pregnancies.

Finally, after Leah had given birth to baby number four, something changed inside her heart. Her response "this time" was different.

> She conceived again, gave birth to a son, and said, *"This time I will praise the Lord."* Therefore she named him Judah. Then Leah stopped having children. (Gen. 29:35, emphasis added)

I want us to lean into these words that Leah's soul whispered. "This time . . ."

I'm not sure her desire to win Jacob's love was the only thing that shifted in her heart. I mean, maybe she did get to the place where she was just plain fed up with him. All these years, all these kids, and he still didn't love her? I would have been over it, that's for sure.

But since her circumstances hadn't changed, since there was no divorce to get, since there were no caring parents or even a sister with a compassionate shoulder on which to have a good cry, I wonder if this shift in perspective came about because she finally saw things for what they really were.

When our circumstances don't change, we only have two choices: settle and pout, or shift and praise. At this point, I think God allowed Leah to see something she needed to see that helped her move on from her comparison struggle.

Disappointment in life is inevitable. And I'm not just talking about a vacation mishap like I shared earlier. Each of us has something we've desired to see happen in our lives that hasn't happened yet. And when we don't see it, yet we see it happening in the lives of others, we often feel the need to strive even harder. Because if *she* can have it, achieve it, or be freed from it, why can't we?

Disappointment is inevitable. But God doesn't want us to settle. He wants us to shift.

I realize this shifting to praise is easier said than done. And while I don't know all the things that might make this choice particularly hard for you, the way it can be hard for me, here's what I do know: God is patient. And while He wants us to get to the place of praise as quickly as possible, He'll still be there even when praising Him doesn't feel possible.

> Disappointment is inevitable. But God doesn't want us to settle. He wants us to shift.

In the meantime, until you get to a place of being able to give God a "this time" praise, I have something to help you. Here are a few *This Time* affirmations for when you're sensing a needed shift in your soul. Read them out loud, claim them over your ache, and let God show you something special.

This Time Affirmations

This time, I will stop looking back at the things I cannot change. I fix my eyes on Jesus because He gives me something to look forward to.

> We do this by keeping our eyes on Jesus, the champion who initiates and perfects our faith. (Heb. 12:2 NLT)

This time, even though my heart aches, I will look for the good things God has given me.

> Devote yourselves to prayer, being watchful and thankful. (Col. 4:2 NIV)

This time, I will go to God's Word instead of the world and believe His promises for me are powerful.

> This is my comfort in my affliction: Your promise has given me life. (Ps. 119:50)

This time, I will look at this unfair situation and seek understanding through wisdom.

> Do you want to be counted wise, to build a reputation for wisdom? Here's what you do: Live

well, live wisely, live humbly. It's the way you
live, not the way you talk, that counts. (James
3:13 MSG)

This time, I will praise the Lord and trust His goodness.

She conceived again, gave birth to a son, and said,
"This time I will praise the LORD." Therefore she
named him Judah. Then Leah stopped having
children. (Gen. 29:35)

The more we affirm God's truth over our lives, the more it
will affect our living.

If none of these affirmations are working for you, write your
own. Affirmations based on God's Word help us hear what we
need in the midst of our own struggles. They help us see things
the way they really are. They remind us who God is and what His
Word says, which can transform us deeply as we surrender to His
truth, His will, and His perspective.

In fact, surrendering to Him might even give you new desires
in place of the old ones.

Seeing Surprises

My friend Amy is a fellow junker. What exactly is a junker?
We are the people who have stickers adorning our car bumpers
that say obnoxious things like, "I brake for yard sales." We also
brake for free items tossed on the curb:

Crates.
Dressers.
Chairs.

Bed frames.

Lamps.

Because everything has potential to us. Everything. *Even donkeys.*

Amy texted me one morning to tell me she was stopping by one of my most favorite junking places, The Old Farmhouse. Junking is always a reason to clear my schedule, so I texted her that I'd be there in a few minutes. I knew I needed some old wooden crates for a project that had been stirring in my head.

But as soon as I crossed the railroad tracks and turned onto the gravel road, I immediately knew something magical was happening. The Old Farmhouse property also houses quite a few animals, and between two fence posts I saw the sweetest little fluffy ears pop up. A perfect baby donkey.

I got out of the car and began to *ooo* and *aah*. Amy smiled and shook her head knowing I was about to be in trouble. I assured her I was just going to take a peek at this little guy with the fluffy, pointy ears, pet him for a minute, and then I'd be on with my crate hunt.

This donkey stood just staring at me, almost calling out to me. It was a gaze that said he'd been waiting his entire life (short as it may have been at that point) to see me. I don't know what his name really was, but "Fred" just felt right to me. I think he liked it too. He came right over to me when I called him that!

Roger, the owner, came out to work some negotiating magic with Amy. A few tables had caught her interest. And so I popped into the negotiation, "Well, what if we bought the baby donkey, too? Fred."

Roger laughed.

Amy laughed.

I wasn't laughing.

So Roger gave me his price, and I gave him a firm, "Sold!"

I had just become a donkey owner.

Which meant I should probably call my husband. That would probably be a good thing. You need to know, at this point in our marriage Kris is quite used to my *"Heeeeeyyyyy, honey"* type phone calls. He knows. He can sniff out the saga as soon as he clicks "answer."

"Let me get this straight," he said. "You went to buy crates and you bought a donkey?!"

"I did! And, honey, I could totally put him in the back of the car. He'd definitely fit!"

Kris made me promise I would not put livestock in the back of our car, but if I could figure out some other way to get him back to our farm, he was fine with it. That's how Fred and his cousin Helen (that's a WHOLE 'NOTHER STORY) came to live with us. And I'm telling you, an excitement welled up in me like nothing I'd ever experienced.

A few years ago, I would never have dreamed that donkeys running across my yard could make me so happy. Living on a farm with a barnyard of misfit animals was never on my fifth-grade list of things I wanted to accomplish.

Mostly, I would never have dreamed of being content with the unique plan that God had written just for me. I don't mean I love His plan every day, especially the ones that involve a marathon of laundry. Some of my old desires still fire up in my soul from time to time, leading me down a comparison black hole.

But when I do feel a "Why her?" rising within me, I've learned to step back, cheer others on, and see the beautiful in others while realizing there's probably some ugly in there too—just like in me.

The surrender of my dreams and desires hasn't been easy. But I've seen a glimpse of the goodness on the other side.

I realize most people reading this book don't have a donkey. Most probably don't want one. But there's something you do want—something that makes your heart sing and come alive when you think about it. The last thing I would ever want to do is tell you to let go of that desire, if it's a good and godly one. I struggle when I meet people whose dreams have seemed to die, their hearts are aching, and they say things like, "Maybe it's just not what God has for me."

Maybe it's not, but maybe it is.

The thing I'd tell you is not to want it based on what others have, not to want it based on a level of striving, not to want it based on the attention it will get from other people, and not to want it based on a false narrative about what really matters in the world. Stop chasing the tails of *maybe now* hopes from one disappointment to the next. Start surrendering to what God truly wants for you in this time, at this place.

> There is always beauty in the midst of our burdens, and a God who blesses us there.

Start looking for the sweet surprises God has in store for you in the midst of situations that are just unfair. I promise He will show them to you. Maybe they're not donkeys, but there is always beauty in the midst of our burdens, and a God who blesses us there. It's up to us to see it.

⁓ This & That ⁓

Wrestle with this:

What is an example of a "maybe now" you've chased?

Remember that:

We need to remember, when looking at people's lives that appear perfect to us, there's probably a not-so-perfect story happening there that's never going to be told.

Desiring things isn't bad, unless our desires become greater than the One who gives desires.

Disappointment is inevitable. But God doesn't want us to settle. He wants us to shift.

Chapter 4

The Other Story

‿

When You Ask: Why Her?
Truth Two: See It Like It Really Is

WE'VE BEEN SEEING THAT THINGS are not always like they seem, how there's always another version to it. And in this story of two comparison-driven sisters married to the same man, the other story is sure to include something unexpectedly surprising. In the last chapter, we saw Leah (the unloved wife) was having babies left and right. Meanwhile, on the other side of the story, Rachel (the one Jacob loved) was yet to become pregnant.

But here we go . . .

When Rachel saw that she was not bearing Jacob any children, she envied her sister. "Give me sons, or I will die!" she said to Jacob. (Gen. 30:1)

Rachel. *Wow.*
Those are some fighting words there.
Jealousy has a way with women's words, doesn't it?
Rachel and Leah. Two sisters. Both craved things out of their control. Each one looked at the other with pain in her heart. Tears in her eyes. And a soul full of misery. But in the last chapter, we

saw Leah make peace with the Lord in her situation. She turned her *maybe now* into a *this time*. She was still in the shadow of her sister, but something had shifted in her for the better.

But Rachel? She's about to take things into her own hands—something that is incredibly dangerous for a woman hosting a spirit of comparison. Comparison can cloud our thinking and cause us to write stories that are not even happening. Which is why the second truth in our *why her* struggle is so vital to grasp: *See it like it really is.*

> Comparison can cloud our thinking and cause us to write stories that are not even happening.

Jacob, in response to Rachel's rant, basically said, *What do you want ME to do about it?* "Am I in the place of God, who has kept you from having children?" (Gen. 30:2 NIV). But Rachel wasn't satisfied with waiting on God. So she had her own idea to control the uncontrollable. She passed off one of her servants to Jacob and demanded that he get her pregnant.

I realize, looking at this story through modern eyes, this practice makes us feel a little uncomfortable. Within their cultural context, however, it was an accepted thing for Jacob to sleep with Rachel's servant. It is what it is. Or, it was what it was.

This same scenario also happened earlier with Sarah (Gen. 16:1–6), when she gave her servant to her husband, Abraham, so he could get this son he'd been promised.

I can't help wondering, though, how Rachel processed the emotional consequences of this sleeping-with-the-servant scheme. Knowing that Jacob slept with her servant? That he was there through the entire pregnancy? That he possibly could start having feelings for this woman?

Oh, mercy.

Let's move on before I blush too much.

So Jacob slept with the servant, she became pregnant, and then Rachel did something quite similar to what we saw from Leah once she conceived.

> Rachel said, "God has vindicated me; yes, he has heard me and given me a son." (Gen. 30:6)

Vindication? Is that seeing it for how it really is?

The word *vindicated* means "to show or prove to be right." Rachel turned what was supposed to be a blessing for herself into a burden for someone else, for Leah. Rachel carried on with this baby battle—even felt so great about how everything was going that she sent Jacob in for round two. "Rachel's slave Bilhah conceived again and bore Jacob a second son" (Gen. 30:7).

Then Rachel pipes up again. And after all the shocking things we've heard so far, what she said following the birth of this second boy *really* shocks me.

> "I have had a great struggle with my sister, and I have won." (Gen. 30:8 NIV)

You've what? You've WON?

Rachel, I don't know about this.

I'm not great at math but according to my simple calculations, Leah had four babies at this point; Rachel had two. So what on earth was making Rachel think she had won this thing?

I have a feeling what Rachel was describing is the fact that she now had the whole package: Jacob's love as well as the two babies.

That's what put her ahead in her mind. But what was *really* happening is that in the process of having these children (even through a side door option), she was introducing a competition into the marriage mix that had no business being there.

Comparison created an unhealthy tension between Rachel and Leah. And even though Leah had called a "this time" time-out to the baby battle, this was not the way it was. The competition wasn't over.

I wish we were only talking about a historical Bible reference here. Wouldn't it be great to say women don't do this kind of stuff to each other anymore? Yet daily we write stories for each other based on what we see from the outside of situations, and we've had other people write stories about us that were not true as well.

You and I have experienced the competitiveness of someone else—ways they were trying to make themselves feel better, feel stronger, feel more ahead of the game. Or maybe we've been the one bringing the competitive disillusionment to the table. (Oh, it just got real quiet, didn't it?)

Comparison's disillusionment begins when we believe our winning makes someone else lose.

But we can begin to see things through more rational eyes once we understand a little better who we really are and who God has made us to be—as well as who *others* are and who He's made *them* to be. Most of the competition we feel and fret over comes from not seeing the true worth that's already been placed in us. Life is not a beauty contest or a power play. It's the discovery of and living out of our unique role in God's purpose.

> Comparison's disillusionment begins when we believe our winning makes someone else lose.

Know Your Place

A few months ago, I was attempting to stay on course as a mom. My oldest daughter, Taylor, and I had been having some normal, mom-daughter struggles, so I was putting forth all the effort I could bring to our relationship. And on a very ordinary Tuesday afternoon, this effort included getting to a school performance *on time*.

I often find myself with a front seat in the "on time" struggle bus. (I'm working on it.) In this case, however—thankfully—we did arrive on time and began walking toward the area where she'd be performing. But I started to feel a little holy sweat rush over me the closer we got, because there at the entrance I saw one of those white folding tables. With a little cream colored cashier box. With a put-together PTO mom guarding the entrance to the event.

Right then I realized I'd either missed the announcement or had never been told that there was a cost for admission. Big fail for a momma who never, ever has cash on her. Give me all the swipes of the debit card, but Lord help me when there's cash involved.

I texted my husband to see if he was almost there. When he responded back with his hour-away, never-gonna-make-it message, I realized I was about to stack another block on my mom failure wall.

A few other parents, who I assumed had also forgotten their cash, were standing off to the side, peeking in. This gave me an idea. I'd get Taylor's attention and let her know I was there, and that I'd be watching from the sidelines. It wasn't ideal, but it would work.

So I told my other two girls to stay put where they were, and I took five steps—seriously, five steps—away from the area where they were collecting the money. Suddenly the PTO Mom Police popped up in front of my face, startling me a little with her stop-right-there command. She proceeded to inform me that I would need to pay five dollars per person in order to walk into said event. I kindly explained that I understood, but I didn't have five dollars in cash. The most I could muster up from my purse would be about seventy-six cents. (Wait . . . one of those pennies had gum stuck to it, so make it seventy-five cents.) I explained that the coordinator for this event hadn't let the parents know there was a cost to enter. Had I known, I would certainly have made sure I'd brought cash with me.

She really didn't seem to care.

So not wanting to start a situation with this woman, I waited till she became occupied again with her paying customers and took a few more steps toward the seating area to see one more time if I could get Taylor's attention.

Just as I stepped in, the PTO Mom Police shouted from her collection post with her sassiest tone, "I mean, if you are going to walk that far, you may as well go in—even though I did just make that little boy right there go find money before he could get in. Go ahead, lady."

The little boy in question, who'd just become the shining example of general admission protocol, looked at me with his *that's-not-fair-she-took-my-concession-candy-money* face. My heart thumped a little faster. So I walked back my five illegal steps and assured her I didn't want to break her rules. I was simply trying to let my daughter know I was there. Could she not understand that? (I didn't actually say that last part.) But after all, I mean, she was a PTO MOM. Wasn't she? Key word: *mom*.

So I never made it into the event. I stood on the sidelines, barely even able to say hello to Taylor. And I was more than mad at this PTO parent. I know there are rules and, trust me, I'm a rule follower. I'm sure, too, there were a thousand unknown reasons to explain her harsh behavior toward me. But I missed a moment with my daughter that day because a woman didn't even try to understand my cashless situation. She must have known how it felt to show up at an event for her kid and not have something go right. Right? (With *her*, maybe not.) She almost seemed to delight in her control over me at that moment.

Kind of reminded me of Rachel's victorious tone toward Leah: "I have won." *Hmph.*

And I guess she did, the PTO mom. She beat me. She won. But I think sometimes we might take our positions a little too far. In our quest for being liked, valued, respected, or in control, we never want to hear the words or be given the impression, "You're not that important." But God is always evaluating our responses, our reactions, and our self-righteous attitudes. And a sure sign that we're turning any relationship or interaction into a "who's more important" competition is when we start to think a little too highly of ourselves.

Neither Rachel nor Leah seemed to know how important they were to the kingdom of God. They were mothering babies who would begin amazing generational lines, the heads of the twelve tribes of Israel. Their little boys would become ancestors to Moses, David, Paul and the other apostles. Amazing men, fulfilling great things God had planned.

Yet with such treasure and blessing cradled in their arms and dancing around their feet, these two sister-wives seemed consumed more with their status. But the status God was writing for them went way beyond what they could see in their moments of comparing and competing.

God is writing a story far beyond anything we can see in the here and now. That's how it really is, not only in *her*, but also in us.

When we do the hard work of letting our faith become top priority, we move into the light where we can see a fuller perspective on what God is doing in each of our lives. We step out of the shadows that are formed by our comparison competition, and we find ourselves balanced in reality.

On one hand, truth tells us not to think of ourselves too highly, understanding that God alone is to be lifted up. One of the things I love most about our office staff at Proverbs 31 Ministries is that no one takes an I'm-too-good-to-do-that position, even when it would be really easy to do so. For example, every week our office manager sends out an email with a list of who's responsible for taking out the trash. Yes, I think at this point in our ministry, we could pay someone to handle the trash. Yet we all take turns. When it's our week to do it, we're on trash duty. No one ever stands up and cheers about it, but we do it. And in doing so, it reminds us, *we're not too good to serve.*

On the other hand, we all must balance out this truth with a companion reality, knowing that God is doing something powerful in and through each one of us personally as His children— things that we know by faith are happening, even when we can't see them.

I wish Rachel could've seen what those words, "I have won," were doing to her big sister. They were causing needless pain, just as Leah's statement, "Surely my husband will love me now," only manufactured more emptiness and comparison in her heart. Both of these women expressed their high-and-mighty stances with God. They each boomeranged their blessing into a burden for the other.

That's not the way it's supposed to be.

God wants to use us. He wants to bless us. But heaven help us when we start to think of our positions as a way to position someone else.

But the good news? He gives us more grace. This is why the Bible says: "God opposes the proud but shows favor to the humble" (James 4.6 NIV). So wherever we find ourselves in the midst of this struggle, there's plenty of grace. And when God gives us the grace we don't deserve, we can freely give it to others.

> God wants to use us. He wants to bless us. But heaven help us when we start to think of our positions as a way to position someone else.

We can see it like it really is.

On-The-Go, Self-Counseling

As a teenager I had the best dog, a golden retriever named Tyler. He was sweet, present, playful, and always up for a car ride. Sadly, Tyler died a few years ago, so we had him cremated and buried him in my parents' backyard.

A few months after Tyler passed away, my older brother had this brilliant idea. He was going to buy our middle daughter, Hope Ann, a puppy for her birthday. And not just any puppy, a golden retriever! I was excited but also a little anxious because a puppy with three kids isn't exactly a suitable ingredient for a clean, sane house. But when we pulled up to the breeder's, the girls got so excited about all the puppies. They were so cute. I mean who can resist a chubby little puppy, especially a golden retriever? So . . .

Princeton the puppy came home with us that day. But he acted nothing like a prince. More like a punk. He dug up our entire backyard. Dragged in mud onto the carpet. Knocked down everything as he trampled through the house. Could never seem to grasp the concept of going potty outside. In one of his later feats, he found the girls' Easter candy in the garage and ate it all. A seven-hundred-dollar vet bill later . . . you get the picture. I felt like the only words I ever said to Princeton were, "Stop it!"

He saved his ultimate mishap, however, for the few weeks when we were living with my parents while waiting to move into our new house. My mom and dad were not fond of Princeton, plus they didn't have a fenced-in backyard. So we tied a long rope around a tree and forced the dog to stay outside as much as possible. He had plenty of room to wander on the rope there. In fact, he seemed to like it—digging just enough to agitate my dad, but mostly behaving himself.

But one afternoon, I heard my dad yelling to me, "Nichole! You better get out here!"

First of all, I know my dad means business if he uses my first name, even to this day. But immediately upon hearing it and rushing outside, I saw he had good reason. All over Princeton's face was some type of gray dust. To my horror I realized, eyeing the place where we'd buried Tyler's ashes, Princeton had dug up my dead dog. *Gasp!*

Needless to say, after that incident, Princeton had to go. We found him a good home, and I'm sure he's the best dog ever . . . *now*. But there are some things that are never meant to be dug up.

And not just ashes.

One of the biggest problems I've noticed with comparison is that I can feel like I'm constantly laying it down, putting it behind me, only to catch myself a few minutes later digging it back up, returning to old mind-sets. The good news, of course, is that God isn't doing the same. I love the picture of Him in this verse:

He has removed our sins as far from us as the east is from the west. (Ps. 103:12 NLT)

Maybe that's why I'm in a season right now where He keeps giving me the same two-word self-counseling to say that I used to say to Princeton daily.

Stop. It.

Why? Because this *why her* struggle is a pattern for me. And I don't want to be in a position of freedom one second and failure the next. So I'm letting these two words boss me around when my soul gets messy.

When I start to doubt my gifts, I say:

Stop. It.

When those little fears of "why not me?" start digging in, I say:

Stop. It.

When I feel jealous as I watch "her" scoot off to this and that opportunity, I say:

Stop. It.

Those two words are not super profound, right? But they are super powerful. When I stop and refuse to dig up these insecurities in me, they allow me to see this situation for what it really is.

What's God revealing that you keep digging back up?

And when you're not *stopping it*—stopping the lies—you need to be doing something else: reminding yourself of the truth.

Auto Fails

If you do any texting at all, you've likely had an autocorrect fail. Wonder how many text messages the autocorrect feature has destroyed? If you Google autocorrect fails, you'll get a good laugh. There are SO many. (Just be sure to add "family-friendly" into that search!)

I think the funniest autocorrect misunderstanding I've personally experienced came from one of my closest friends, Wendy. She sent me a question about taking my daughter Taylor on a trip to Disney with her and with someone named "Kevin Ziering." Hmm. Had a few questions about that. First, who is Kevin Ziering? And second (whoever he is), why would Wendy think I'd let her take Taylor to Disney with some boy I'd never met? She knows me well enough to know I would not be okay with that scenario. *Or maybe she didn't know me as well as I thought she did!* I hesitated a bit in responding.

A few minutes later she texted me again, "I don't know who Kevin Ziering is, but he is *not* coming to Disney with me! Stupid autocorrect!" We both sent the laughing face emoji, and I breathed a sigh of relief.

But our brains can write inaccurate stories just as effectively as autocorrect can.

If we've written a story about ourselves or about God that isn't true, and if we've done it for an extended period of time, our brains may have started to believe it. Even if we know the truth and understand who God is, our brains may not have caught up with our hearts yet. The same way our phones automatically correct the texts we type, our brains can do the same thing. So when we're confronting a comparison issue that we've faced over and over, it's easy for us to write the same, hopeless story in our minds.

We need to train our minds to "get it"—to see it like it really is. And one of the ways I do it is with some repeated reminders. While I could probably think of at least a dozen things we need to remind ourselves of each day, I've broken it down to these two because too much can easily lead to brain overload. And if your brain is like mine, we're close to it.

Here they are:

1. God's goodness
2. Who you are becoming

God's Goodness

God is a good God. And daily we need to remind ourselves that His goodness is all around. We need to see it, say it, believe it, and receive it for our lives. When circumstances are unfair and our hearts are aching, God is still concerned that we learn to experience His goodness. And the words that pass through our mouths in those moments will reflect if we're seeing

> When circumstances are unfair and our hearts are aching, God is still concerned that we learn to experience His goodness.

71

it or not. This is my favorite verse to quote when I need to see God's goodness and be grateful for it.

> Surely your goodness and love will follow me all the days of my life, and I will dwell in the house of the LORD forever. (Ps. 23:6 NIV)

Who You Are Becoming

If we don't love who we were yesterday, we can at least love who we have the opportunity to become today. Each day is filled with new opportunities for beauty, creativity, and life. Sure, there were some things I didn't love about myself yesterday. There were some *why her* thoughts I entertained. But I don't have to let yesterday be my story for today. When I need to remember this process, I pull out this verse:

> Remember not the former things, nor consider the things of old. Behold, I am doing a new thing; now it springs forth, do you not perceive it? I will make a way in the wilderness and rivers in the desert. (Isa. 43:18–19 ESV)

I really believe as we keep these two things front and center of our lives each day, we give ourselves the best chance for God to author the greatest story for our lives. It's not always like it seems. But it also doesn't have to be like it seems.

> It's not always like it seems. But it also doesn't have to be like it seems.

You still with me? If so, here's a fun assignment: Send me a tweet @NickiKoziarz with this: Still with you. #WhyHerBook

I can't wait to virtually high-five you!
See you in chapter 5!

～ This & That ～

Wrestle with this:

What is an example of how comparison can create the disillusionment of "winning"?

Remember that:

Comparison's disillusionment begins when we believe our winning makes someone else lose.

God wants to use us. He wants to bless us. But heaven help us when we start to think of our positions as a way to position someone else.

When circumstances are unfair and our hearts are aching, God is still concerned that we learn to experience His goodness.

Truth Three

You Don't Always Have to Be Okay

Chapter 5

Three Great Decisions

⌒

When You Ask: Why Her?
Truth Three: You Don't Always Have to Be Okay

MY YOUNG FRIEND'S HEART WAS shattered.

A guy she'd been dating for six months had decided to break up with her, but he didn't even have the decency to do it face-to-face. He did it over texting. *Ugh.* It was a sudden blow, popping up out of nowhere. And as we sat together in a corner at a coffee shop, I listened as she processed her tears, shock, and disbelief.

A few days prior to our talk, she'd discovered the reason behind this shift in his feelings. There was another "her." And so my friend began that awful *why her* comparison struggle. First, she opened up the woman's Instagram account to scrutinize her pictures. She investigated how many friends she had on Facebook. Asked Google for more details about her. Then kept digging, trying to answer the ultimate *why her* question: What did this woman have that she didn't? But the search only led her to more breakdowns, which only led to more bitterness. She was not okay with this. With *any* of this.

And she shouldn't have been.

While my friend was talking, I kept thinking about Leah. It wasn't exactly the same situation, but it was within the same thread.

When Rachel said, "I have won" (Gen. 30:8 NIV), after God had given her a two-baby blessing, was Leah okay? Could Rachel have said such harsh words without a look of uttermost satisfaction dancing across her face? It must have stirred something inside of Leah. Do you think she didn't shed some tears after that? Felt like arguing? Wanted to vent her frustrations to Jacob? To somebody?

Life is going to try breaking us down. No matter how much we love God, there are going to be people, situations, problems, and heartbreaks that come along which are still incredibly hard to handle. But when life breaks us down, we always have two options.

Bitterness or Breakthrough

None of us wants to walk through these painful comparison struggles and end up bitter. We all desire to have breakthrough. But when we've experienced a loss of trust, confidence, peace, and relationship, we'll sometimes do whatever it takes to make ourselves feel okay again.

We'll resort to fighting back, making others pay for what they've done to us. We'll do things that actually work against the breakthrough God wants to give us.

This is what it seems like Leah did. When pushed hard enough by Rachel's high-and-mighty stance about these sons God had given her, Leah decided to crank things up a notch, and fight fire with fire.

When Leah saw that she had stopped having children, she took her slave Zilpah and gave her to Jacob as a wife. Leah's slave Zilpah bore Jacob a son. Then Leah said, "What good fortune!" and she named him Gad. (Gen. 30:9–11)

But doesn't this all feel a bit confusing? Leah stopped having children. Then Rachel said, "I have won." So Leah sends her servant to Jacob to get pregnant.

We watched Leah initially chasing all those *maybe now* thoughts while her first three babies were being born, even though none of them led her to a place where Jacob finally loved her. Then we saw her beautiful surrender—"This time I will praise the LORD" (Gen. 29:35). She turned her struggle into praise. So I kind of thought Leah had experienced some healing from this. Didn't you?

But then, for some reason, she decided to pick it up all over again, which gives us another peek into her soul. *She still wasn't okay.* And another baby breakdown came. The breakdown seemed to have turned into bitterness.

I think this is a good place to introduce the third truth that helps lessen our *why her* struggles.

Truth Three: You Don't Always Have to Be Okay

We live in a culture that teaches women they need to be seen as strong. And yes, strength is a needed value for God's women. We can't walk around defeated and depleted all the time. But the admitting of our not-being-okay sometimes comes with a heavy blanket of comparison wrapped around it. Because admitting this? That we're not okay? It could make us seem weak. Especially as we look at *her*.

But the faking of being fine when met with another woman's competitive spirit can stir up a breakdown faster than anything else.

I think we might know why.

You knew this was coming, right? We have to talk about it. Yes. So sorry.

The problem at the core of this comparison struggle between Rachel and Leah (as well as most every other comparison struggle) was *jealousy*. And before we get all, "Look at this horrible case of jealousy in the Bible!" I think we first need to admit a few things about ourselves.

I have yet to ever meet a woman who didn't struggle with some sort of jealousy in her life. Sometimes it's only enough to make her say, "Well, *that's* not fair." But other times I've seen jealousy completely ruin people, relationships, and even God-assignments.

Jealousy found me at such an early age. Maybe for you too?

As a young girl, I wasn't the prettiest peach. I mentioned earlier that we didn't have a lot of money, so my clothes were often hand-me-downs. Plus, I had horribly crooked teeth. And I couldn't see well, which everyone else learned the afternoon my eye doctor put pink, plastic, Coke-bottle glasses on my face. I was also an '80s baby, so I had one of those moms who made the tragic agreement for a perm, which really just created one giant frizz ball on my head. Hot-mess-express was the unwritten (yet known) description next to my yearbook pictures.

I was constantly comparing. And constantly jealous. *Seventeen* magazine fed me the tips on beauty and body image that supposedly made the difference between me and everyone else who looked way more put-together than I did. But no matter how hard I tried, "Most Beautiful" was never going to be my superlative.

Many afternoons I remember sitting and crying in my New Kids On The Block poster-filled room (my favorite boy band), absolutely hating my reflection in the mirror. I'd stare at Jordan Knight, Donnie Wahlberg, and Joey McIntyre, knowing they'd never pick me out from a crowd at their concert to stand on a stage and sing "Cover Girl" to me. But a girl could still dream, couldn't she?

Eventually, of course, I grew out of it. I got contacts for my nearsightedness, braces for my smile, a straightener for my frizzy hair, and a job so I could buy my own clothes, all of which greatly improved my outside appearance. But the inside was still a fragile, ugly-duckling girl who was jealous of others all the time. And it ruined so much of who I was, because I was always looking at who I wasn't.

Sometimes, even today as a grown woman, this same fragile place can still be stirred within me. When life mistreats me and I'm *not okay*, I need to be more accepting rather than rejecting of these raw places. Because when I try to move on too quickly, the breakdown almost always comes.

So I get why Leah could so easily pick back up this battle of hers. Sometimes for me, all it takes is one comment, one rejection, one moment of looking at someone else for my eyes to turn from blue to green. Jealousy slips back in. The breakthrough is gone and bitterness wins.

Before we move on to some of the things we feel threatened or outmatched or discontented about, in comparison with others, let's take a deep breath and have a real, honest conversation about this.

While we can't get rid of comparison, we can certainly weaken this internal enemy of jealousy with a better understanding. I think once we know its physical, emotional, and spiritual impacts, we can come up with a game plan to strengthen our souls.

Here are a few things I've discovered about the various effects of jealousy.

Physical Effects of Jealousy

- Crying
- Increased pulse
- Sweating
- Stomach in knots
- Shaking/trembling
- Illness
- Twitching
- Losing sleep
- Nightmares

Emotional Effects of Jealousy

- Decrease of self-worth
- Emotional instability
- Constant feelings of bitterness
- Prolonged depression
- Extreme anxiety
- Victim mentality
- Troubled relationships
- Consistent feeling of panic

Spiritual Effects of Jealousy

- Self-centered approach with God ("What about me?")
- Hindrances in praying

- Distrust of God
- Distractions from your own God-assignments
- Enhanced fear

Some of these effects arise only from extreme cases of jealousy, but if you're experiencing any of these symptoms, it's time to pay attention. Take notice of the positions in your heart that don't feel okay. They may be signs of jealousy that have crept in while you've been living with the idea that you're always supposed to be okay, instead of being able to honestly admit, "This really stinks right now."

Because sometimes it just does.

I've come to understand something about these feelings. *They change*—some days more frequently than others. I've learned to press pause on any of these effects of jealousy I feel in given moments, realizing emotions are temporary, but actions and words are permanent.

We don't know all the effects this comparison battle brought out in Rachel and Leah, other than the fact that their words became weapons, their blessings became burdens, and their struggles never seemed to stop. But whether the jealousy in your life is as extreme as theirs or is more of a little side note, either can be dangerous because it always has the potential to escalate into something more. If not kept in check, the jealousy of comparison can become a wheel of destruction that never stops spinning.

> Emotions are temporary, but actions and words are permanent.

The Community We Need

Being okay all the time is simply not realistic. That's not our goal. Nor is it a reality in anyone else's life either. It's not the way it really is. Exposing our own weakness toward jealousy and allowing God to overcome its damaging effects on us is a significant step in our freedom.

> Exposing our own weakness toward jealousy and allowing God to overcome its damaging effects on us is a significant step in our freedom.

But while we're deliberately digging up these deep roots of jealousy, we should also be doing something else of even greater importance—planting our roots even deeper in community.

God designed us with a desire for community. Comparison convinces us that community doesn't exist for us. When we're learning to combat comparison, it's easy to walk into a room full of people and see everything we're not. *She* will be there . . . the prettier, smarter, wealthier, more likeable one.

And comparison will whisper these lies: *You don't belong here. You're not good enough. These aren't your people.*

Believing the lies makes sliding out of face-to-face community a frequent happening. It's safer to live together through our screens, we think—through Facebook statuses and technological togetherness. Our scrolls convince us we're connecting with others.

But when we're not okay, we need to be able to tell it to someone who loves us, cares for us, and wants something better for us. We need the kind of community we've built through careful acts of intentionality. We need trusted voices with whom we can entrust our soul struggles, people we can call or visit in person when someone says something to us that isn't what our soul needs to hear. We need friends and fellow believers who give us a solid place to go and lay down our "I'm not okay." Because I've learned something from experience: Not everyone should be a trusted voice in our lives.

The Right Wisdom

Several years ago, these exact words—"I'm not okay"—had become twisted around my heart. I'd been fighting it, but if you'd asked me at the time if my soul was well, the answer was no. I didn't think there was anything specific happening in my current life situation to create such a level of discontent in my soul. I wondered if there was something from my past lingering. Because often comparison will use the pain of our past to create problems in our present.

I'd also just started becoming more aware of my own struggle with comparison, so this issue was there to greet me around every corner. And I suspect, since you've stuck around here with me to nearly the halfway point of this book, the same thing is possibly happening to you. This comparison, as you know, can make a woman's heart miserable. I guess you could say misery found *me*.

> Often comparison will use the pain of our past to create problems in our present.

I knew I needed to talk to someone about the struggles and strains of my soul. So I did it. I looked at my calendar and created the space to seek counsel from someone I assumed would be wise, helpful, and discerning. I thought we would be on the same page regarding what I was looking for and what I truly needed.

About fifteen minutes into our conversation, I had laid all my soul struggles out across the table. They were sitting there one by one, waiting to be covered in hope, joy, and peace. But I didn't seem to be getting back the wisdom from her that I'd paid for. Instead, I found myself climbing a mountain of questionable questions.

The main tip-off that told me something was wrong was that although I'd barely mentioned my husband, Kris, this counselor kept pressing me for more depth on him, while I kept steering the conversation back around to the struggles I'd already shared. After all, *these* were the struggles that were creating my misery, not *him*. I'm not saying our marriage is perfect, but all the things I'd stacked on the table had absolutely nothing to do with Kris. That much I knew.

By the end of our appointment, however, she had a grand solution for all my misery: *leave my husband.* Trust me, my mouth dropped too. In fact, when I shared my shock about it with someone else a few weeks later, I heard that "leaving your husband" was one of this counselor's common prescriptions for women's problems—most likely stemming from her own broken marriage that had left her in a bitter place. But how could someone who knew me for less than sixty minutes make such a declaration? The "wisdom" she was giving me was nothing like what the book of James describes.

> The wisdom from above is first pure, then peace-loving, gentle, compliant, full of mercy and good fruits, unwavering, without pretense. (James 3:17)

I'm a big fan of counseling as a way of receiving unbiased truth in our lives. In fact, I didn't let this initial episode make me give up on it. A few phone calls later, I was able to find a counselor who helped me sort through my table of struggles, walking out the hard, messy journey toward freedom with me. But the closer we stay to trusted people in our everyday community, the more we'll receive the kind of wisdom we can count on.

> There's a time to seek counsel, but there's also no substitute for community.

There's a time to seek counsel, but there's also no substitute for community. We need it. And there are people who need us. God's Word reassures our wandering hearts that the church needs what each of us was created to do in order for it to be fully functional.

> For just as each of us has one body with many members, and these members do not all have the same function, so in Christ we, though many, form one body, and each member belongs to all the others. (Rom. 12:4–5 NIV)

Bodies can still function without a finger, a toe, or even an arm or a leg. But it's challenging. And it's the same within the church. We can learn to get by on our own, but missing out on the kind of support we are designed for could keep us just barely surviving. God created us with a need for one another.

> God created us with a need for one another. He didn't give the choir a lifetime assignment of solos.

He didn't give the choir a lifetime assignment of solos. He made us to function together.

While it's incredibly important that you and I get to the place where we can honestly say the words, "I'm not okay," we also need to know who we can trust to speak into our lives. Don't let just anyone into this private place. Guard your heart carefully to be sure you gain the right understanding.

But doing this requires community. Not *perfect* community. Even the church, we know, is filled with flawed and fragile people. But they are worth the risk when they offer those things that James 3:17 describes—peace, gentleness, mercy, and authenticity.

Wisdom.

I'll confess something to you. I can count on one hand the friends I would call in a time of chaos or crisis. I have plenty of acquaintances, professional relationships, and teammates. But when it comes down to baring my soul and admitting I'm not okay, there are very, very few people who hold that position in my life. Community has been painful for me in the past. I'm still learning what it means to build it.

> Guard your heart carefully to be sure you gain the right understanding.

But I don't want the pain of the past to make me miss out on the promise of now. And if you feel the same way, I hope through this process you gain the encouragement to try again. Maybe you need to take it slowly, like me. I've learned community doesn't need to be big. In some moments, I have to remind myself to just keep going. There's nothing wrong with taking community slow as long as we're taking steps toward it and not away from it.

I hope Leah and Rachel both had a trusted community outside of what seemed such an unhappy home. I hope someone in Leah's life told her to reject those hurtful words that Rachel spoke. I hope someone gave her wise counsel on how misery loves to multiply, and how those words of Rachel's came from her own struggle, not Leah's. And at those times when Leah was the one who was spreading bitterness through her words, I hope Rachel had a community outside of her home environment, too, that spoke truth and encouragement to her.

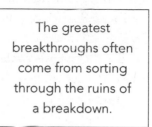

The greatest breakthroughs often come from sorting through the ruins of a breakdown.

And I hope you trust me today when I tell you it's okay if you're not okay right now. But there's something else I've learned along the way that perhaps you also need to hear: The greatest breakthroughs often come from sorting through the ruins of a breakdown.

Break It Down

Do you remember my friend I told you about—the one who'd been jilted via text message? I was thankful she reached out to me as part of her community that day, and continued to do so for several days afterward. She needed an in-real-life person sitting in her physical presence or talking with her on the phone who could let her know it was okay not to be okay.

But there came a point when I knew we needed to shift things. So after talking about this situation with her for the umpteenth time, I tried to help her *break it down,* instead of staying *broken down.*

When we're in a position of not feeling okay, there's a time to climb out from under the bedcovers. I know it's where we feel like staying sometimes, but if we want the *breakdown* to lead to the *breakthrough,* we need to get up and actually go through it.

Hopefully, you're not going through a relationship breakdown right now. But maybe you are. Even if you're not, I'm sure there's something else that's got you sifting through the ruins—trouble with your job, a longing, a desire, a dream—something that's causing you to whisper under your breath, *I'm not okay.* Whatever it is, or whenever it comes, here are three decisions I helped my broken-hearted friend sort through which can help lead you to the breakthrough.

Decision One: Choose God's Promises

> Let us hold tightly without wavering to the hope we affirm, for God can be trusted to keep his promise. (Heb. 10:23 NLT)

Yes, it's okay not to always be okay.

But it's *not* okay to *NEVER* be okay.

That's not what God wants for us. He needs us to know He's a good God who has good things for our lives. In fact, He wants us to be more than just okay. His Word is filled with so much power and authority, with so many examples and clear statements of His goodness. It is good to say, "God is good," but it is better to know God's goodness.

> It is good to say, "God is good," but it is better to know God's goodness.

If we'll live with these promises and pray them over the non-okay portions of our lives, we'll soon not only be *saying*, "God is good," but we will actually be applying and experiencing and coming to understand the reality of His goodness. Staying in the truth of His Word is essential to breakthrough.

I know a lot of people who pick one specific life-verse to claim over themselves consistently, which is a great thing to do. But we need more than one verse. We need a whole army of them! So here's a chart filled with verses to look up, read, and maybe even write down to carry with you when you need a promise to hold tightly.

Psalm 16:11	Isaiah 58:9–10	Romans 4:21
Psalm 85:8	Jeremiah 31:33–34	Hebrews 6:13–18
Psalm 110:4a	John 1:12	2 Peter 1:3–4
Psalm 145:13b	John 16:22–24	1 John 1:9

Look up these verses and circle the promises you're holding on to for your life. Write out at least one of them below.

_____

_____

_____

Decision Two: Fight for God's Promises

"A thief comes only to steal and kill and destroy. I have come so that they may have life and have it in abundance." (John 10:10)

God's promises are not only for reading and meditating on. There are times when we must fight to believe them and receive them for our lives. No, I don't mean my friend should have gone and knocked out the woman who stole her boyfriend. But he had taken something else from her, her heart. And now it was time to fight for it and bring it closer to the One who heals the brokenhearted.

What loss are you feeling the most through this struggle of comparison?

- Identity?
- Confidence?
- Joy?
- Peace?

Whatever it is, if God's clearly given you a promise for it, it's time to take it back. As John 10:10 reminds us, we have an Enemy who wants to steal everything from us, especially God's promises. But the more time you spend in the Word, the Holy Spirit will cause specific verses to stand out and become key weapons in your fight.

When God's Word tells us He wants us to experience abundance in our lives, He means it.

- Abundance of identity that points back to Him
- Abundance of confidence in who He created us to be
- Abundance of joy that overflows our souls
- Abundance of peace to calm our fears

Abundance. God doesn't do anything halfway.

So, what are you taking back today? Write it below. (And if you already know of a specific Bible promise related to this situation, write it down too.)

_____

_____

_____

Decision Three: Walk in Truth

"You will know the truth, and the truth will set you free."
(John 8:32)

Recently, I had a conversation with someone I didn't know very well. They were asking me all kinds of hard questions, and I felt like they were trying to back me into a corner. What they really wanted to know was my opinion about one or more cultural struggles that are pressing and controversial today.

As this intense conversation progressed, I realized something. While I did have opinions about these things, my opinions don't really matter. Because when you decide you're going to live a life based on the truth of God, opinions aren't worth a lot. Truth is truth. And my opinion only matters to the degree that it lines up with biblical truth.

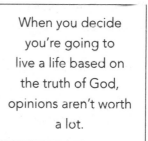

When you decide you're going to live a life based on the truth of God, opinions aren't worth a lot.

For years I've wrestled with God about many things. And you know what? He has never resisted my wrestling. My questions, my doubts, my fears, my many, many wonderings—He's more than tolerated them all. But through all the wrestling, I've found a resting place with God. Because regardless of the situation or topic or struggle, His truth remains.

It is often our wrestling with God that leads us to the resting place of God.

So when I'm not okay, I know it's time to start wrestling with truth. Many people see God's truth as a prison but, oh my goodness, it's quite the opposite. It's the place of freedom. In His truth is where we can rest and stop trying to figure it all out.

These three decisions help us transition from breakdown to breakthrough:

1. Choose God's Promises
2. Fight for God's Promises
3. Walk in Truth

Next time you feel the beginning of a breakdown, remember these decisions. Hang them on your mirror. Post them on social media. Do whatever you need to do to keep your soul away from bitterness.

I don't want to be like Rachel, spewing out things I shouldn't say. And I also don't want to be like Leah, picking up the battle again and again. I want to realize, when I'm feeling a little broken, that it's okay not to be okay. And I want to make decisions that lead me to breakthrough, not bitterness. I'm sure that's what you want too.

And I say we do it together.

⁓ This & That ⁓

Wrestle with this:

Who are your handful of trusted people? If you don't have anyone yet, write out a prayer to God asking Him to show you.

Remember that:

Exposing our own weakness toward jealousy and allowing God to overcome its damaging effects on us is a significant step in our freedom.

Often comparison will use the pain of our past to create problems in our present.

God created us with a need for one another. He didn't give the choir a lifetime assignment of solos.

Chapter 6

How's Your Soul?

When You Ask: Why Her?
Truth Three: You Don't Always Have to Be Okay

HOW ARE YOU? LIKE, REALLY.

Maybe your honest answer to this question is, "I'm not okay." Hopefully, as we're working through this third truth regarding the *why her* struggle, you're more comfortable now with the reality that "you don't always have to be okay." But just as it's necessary to be able to say we're not okay, it's also essential for us to know how to keep our souls well.

That's why, if we were meeting in person right now, I probably wouldn't ask you the question I led this chapter with—"How are you?" I *hate* that question. Mmm, maybe "hate" is too strong a word. But I really dislike it. It feels so fake.

Would I ever *really* tell someone how I'm doing, in such a hi-how-are-you, passing-by type of conversation? *No.* And most likely, neither would you. In fact, maybe that's why we ask it of other people so often—because we don't really care enough to know.

There are times, however, when I really *do* want to know what's going on with someone. So when the time is right, I've started asking this question: *"How's your soul?"*

I've been amazed watching how this question opens up the window to someone's heart. Sometimes people tense up when I ask it, but other times their body language totally relaxes. It's like they finally feel comfortable to step past the layers of not-okay denial.

So let's try this again. "What do you think it would take for you today to be able to say your soul is well?"

Each time comparison turns into jealousy, and from there turns into bitterness, our souls get a little more unwell. It prevents us from living confidently in who God created us to be. We've seen it happening throughout the story of Rachel and Leah. They both needed someone to look them straight in the eye and ask, "How's your soul?"

> "What do you think it would take for you today to be able to say your soul is well?"

Simply asking this question makes us pause. Reflect. And it gives us the opportunity to get rid of the things that are not making us well.

Recently, I texted a few friends and asked them, "How do you know when your soul is not well?" While I know what a few of my own unwell soul clues are, I was curious to know theirs. See if you can identify with any of their responses:

- "I become numb to my feelings and emotions."
- "I act out of character. I blame everybody but me (in my head) and I'm usually restless."
- "My temper is quick and I have feelings of unrest."

- "I feel anxious. I start trying to do things in my own strength."
- "I become irritable and impatient. I avoid people. And I start to make excuses for not following through with things."
- "I'm defensive and critical."
- "My thoughts and words quickly get to a bad place."

I could identify with each of these unwell soul clues and, most likely, so can you. Based on these quotes, I compiled a list of things that might even say it a little more clearly. See if you spot your unwell soul clues as we look at them this way:

- Losing your temper quickly
- Believing lies
- Responding harshly
- Lacking grace/empathy
- Making judgments
- Spending too much time on social media
- Crying frequently
- Always stressed out
- Not being able to see the good in things
- Working all the time
- Thinking the worst before assuming the best
- Not being able to turn your brain off
- Gossiping
- Consuming too much food, TV, Netflix
- Lying
- Covering up mistakes
- Not being able to apologize
- Pulling back from community/church

I don't know if any of these represent your unwell soul clues or not, but I want you to think about what yours might be so you can learn to recognize them before they become toxic. Keep them in the back of your mind.

And if you're still a little unclear on which ones are the most challenging, Scripture gives us the most analytical test of all.

Listen for the Clues

While God is the only one who can truly see what's happening inside of us, we can listen for it. Jesus spoke to this very thing when He said . . .

> "What comes out of the mouth comes from the heart, and this defiles a person." (Matt. 15:18)

When Jesus shared these words, He was speaking to a dispute between the Pharisees and Jesus' disciples about the subject of ritually washing their hands before they ate. (Makes me wonder what Jesus would say about most of our arguments today, as well as the many comparisons we make with others. "So silly. Stop it.") But through this teaching, Jesus was reminding His followers that you can tell a lot more about a person's heart by what's coming *out* of their mouths than by what's going *in*.

Jesus was always most concerned with the heart. And the words we say—"what comes out of the mouth"—are a good clue to the condition of our heart. They reflect for us how things are going in our soul.

I often don't even realize how unwell my soul has become until I hear myself saying something that makes me feel instantly sick. Have I said some things in my life I've regretted? Absolutely.

Rachel and Leah? They said some things that had the potential to leave some regret marks too.

- "I have won!"
- "God has vindicated me!"
- "Give me babies or I will die!"

Jealousy, pride, hurt, and insecurity can make a woman spew things out of her mouth she would like to take back. Our words tell us something.

So listen to yourself.

What are you hearing?

Life gives all of us a story to tell, but the response of our words reveals if our souls are unwell.

My friend Chrystal was the first person to tell me about this app called Voxer, sort of a walkie-talkie thing that lets you send voice memos to people. I told her I'd give it a try but I wasn't sure I'd be hooked. Well, after a few messages back and forth with her, I loved it! It's a great way to keep communication open with friends both near and far. You can hear each other's voices, send longer messages than the typical text, and communicate verbally without having to schedule phone calls.

One of the things I love about Voxer is you can go back and listen to the entire conversation again. Unlike a live conversation, where words can be quickly forgotten, words spoken on Voxer are there for a really long time. And they can be replayed over and over.

But I've found it's also a great tool for something else—like, when I'm trying to listen in for my *own* soul-is-not-well clues.

Sometimes if I've sent a message I'm not too sure I should have sent, I go back and listen to it. I can hear what I said, hear the words I chose to use, and hear the tone in which I said them. Sometimes I feel confident about the way I spoke, but other times I immediately clue into the fact that something in my soul isn't well.

I realize, of course, we can't all go around Voxing every conversation we have. Life doesn't work that way. But even in real time—especially in real time—we do need to listen to what we're saying, how we're saying it, and what kind of effect it's having on the people around us. When a woman learns to listen to her unwell soul clues, she will become much less likely to let the struggle of comparison ruin her.

What kind of clues is your soul giving you today? Lean in, listen, and learn to catch those clues before they become regretful words.

Soul-Care Strategy

One thing I've come to understand about my soul is this: I'm the only one who can take care of it. Yes, God can place the kindest, most generous people around me to help care for my soul, but ultimately it's up to me to do it.

Sometimes my soul gives me clues that it's not well, like when I notice myself reaching toward other things, opportunities, and people to fill the space within me that only God can fill. Maybe you notice those kinds of patterns and habits in yourself too. That's when we need a soul-care strategy—a plan of sorts to push us toward breakthrough.

> One thing I've come to understand about my soul is this: I'm the only one who can take care of it.

I've developed a soul-care strategy of my own that helps me shift from not being okay to becoming well again. It's made up of three components:

1. Identify Your Three Ns
2. Find Your Happy
3. Catalog Your Compliments

I realize what's worked for me may not be the perfect fit for you. But maybe it will help get you going in the right direction. Let's work through this together so you can have your own soul-care strategy.

Soul-Care Strategy, Part One: Identify Your Three Ns

First N: Identify the Noise

I'm amazed at how much our culture resists quiet. Most of our days are spent managing noise—noise from others, noise from our technology, noise from our inner thoughts. We may even fall asleep at night to the noise of a sound machine or with the TV on (guilty as charged). Sometimes it feels like there's so much going on in my head that I can't even hear myself think, let alone hear God. When it seems like God is quiet, we need to get quiet.

What have you heard today? Talking? Shouting? Crying? Horns blowing? Phone dings?

> When it seems like God is quiet, we need to get quiet.

Better question: Has there been a moment of silence in your life today?

If the answer is no, put this book down right now and just let yourself de-noise for a minute or two. When my soul is giving me a clue that it's not well, even just getting quiet and still for a few moments helps me recognize where I'm struggling.

I want you to identify the areas of your life that are the loudest right now. Determine what makes it so loud and what you need to do to quiet your soul. Try capturing your thoughts on this subject in the lines below, or expand on them in a notebook or journal.

_____

_____

_____

Second N: Identify Notifications

Once we discover the importance of allowing a little bit of silence in our lives, we become incredibly sensitive to noise. One of the first steps I took when I became more aware of this was turning off almost every notification on my phone. The days my soul seems to be the most unwell are the days when my phone buzzes and dings all day long.

I still remember the moment when I discovered that I could silence group text messages. It was one of the most glorious days of my life. Turning off this notification doesn't make all the messages go away. They're still there. But I can go back later—when I have the mental capacity for it—and look at the many responses a group message can bring in.

Every couple of weeks I also take a few minutes to go through my emails and unsubscribe to at least five or six of those daily subscriptions that somehow include my email address. This helps clear my inbox so it doesn't feel so overwhelming every day.

Most notifications tend to be a nuisance. But one way notifications have *helped* keep my soul well is by alerting me to the most important things I need to remember each day. I'm a forgetful one by nature, and when life becomes too full I start forgetting meetings, phone calls, and appointments, which leads my soul to become incredibly unwell.

What are some notifications you need to remove? What are some you need to keep? And what are some you may need to add?

Third N: Identify Nosiness

Oh yes, here we go. How much information is too much information?

Most days I scroll through my social media feed simply out of curiosity. *What are you up to? What did you eat for lunch? How's your dog today? Can I please see your baby laugh again?*

But honestly, do we really need to know so much about each other? The world was spinning just fine before social media appeared on the scene and began inviting us into every single moment of each other's lives.

Do you follow people on social media who you really aren't that close to? Would your life be any less-than by not keeping up with them? Maybe it's time to un-follow them. Not to be rude. Not to be mean. But simply to simplify your need to know.

How's your nosiness level? Are you good? Or do you need to take it down a notch?

_____

_____

_____

Soul-Care Strategy, Part Two: Find Your Happy

There is something that makes me laugh like nothing else in this world. And you are probably going to think it's the *dumbest* thing in the world, I just know it. But I'm telling you anyway.

There's a pug on YouTube. His name is Ozzy. (You love him already, don't you?) And Ozzy does not like to get in his bed. No matter how many times his owner gives the command, he doesn't listen. He even says, "I WON'T!"

I'm not kidding, go watch it.

Ozzy's video has over four million views, and I assure you I have contributed greatly to that number! I've watched this video so many times I know the entire thing by heart. In fact, I'm giggling while I'm writing this now, just thinking about it—because Ozzy makes me laugh so hard I cry almost every time I watch him.

I know it's just a silly video. It really is. And no one else in my family thinks it's even remotely funny. But for some reason, that pug makes me laugh like no one else can.

Why am I telling you this story? Because sometimes we just need to find our happy again. *Our* happy. Not what makes everyone else smile, giggle, or laugh. Just us. Even if it's just for a moment.

If your soul is feeling unwell, here's your charge—go find laughter. You need it.

What is that thing that makes you laugh like nothing else?

_____

_____

_____

Soul-Care Strategy, Part Three: Catalog Your Compliments

Do you remember the first real compliment you ever got? I don't mean the ones your parents or your teachers gave you. I'm referring to a moment when someone you didn't know or someone you'd just met oozed something nice about you.

I'll tell you one that stands out to me. Before the day of phone cameras—which take better pictures than *real* cameras took seventeen years ago—people often took their kids to portrait studios and got professional photos made. I wish I'd have had the funds to do that more when my girls were little. But one time when I was really wanting some black-and-white pictures of my daughter Taylor, off to the drug store we went. Because y'all, I had to buy FILM. I know . . . *FILM*.

I put Taylor in her loveliest pink-flowered dress, plopped a big pink bow on her head, and sat her in front of the fireplace. This, my friend, was the extent of her very first photo shoot.

A few days later I took the film back to the same drug store to get it developed. I realize, if you're in your twenties or younger, you're like, *you did WHAT?* Trust me. You couldn't just put the pictures straight onto your computer then. But it wasn't really so bad. It only took one hour to get our film developed. (Google it, Generation Z, it was a thing.)

As I stood at the counter waiting to pick up my pictures, an older gentleman who looked like he'd lived a good bit of life and knew a thing or two about his job brought them to me. "Did you take these?" he asked as he handed me the pictures. Embarrassed that maybe he was about to offer me a photographer's phone number to help me out in the future, I shyly nodded my head. But then he said something I'll never forget: "I've seen a lot of pictures, honey. These are good. *Really* good."

To tell you the truth, I cannot remember what I ate for dinner last night. That moment in the drug store was seventeen years ago, and I can still see the expression on his face and hear those words.

The power of a compliment.

Today in our selfie world, authentic compliments are such a rare thing. Sure, we "like" our lives away on social media. But when was the last time you stopped and said something really nice to someone? We can't live our lives dependent on the praise of someone else, but we can live our lives daily praising others.

> We can't live our lives dependent on the praise of someone else, but we can live our lives daily praising others.

Catalog your compliments—the ones people say to you, and the ones you think of and need to share with others, blessing *them* with a compliment as well. Remember those tender, nice, unexpected moments, and pull them back out when you need them. It will do your soul well to remember them, and also to give them.

What is the nicest thing someone has ever said to you?

_____

_____

_____

The next time your soul is feeling a little less-than, pull out this strategy and let it be a tool to encourage you.

1. Identify Your Three Ns
2. Find Your Happy
3. Catalog Your Compliments

Simple Things

Taking care of our souls doesn't mean we put all of our responsibilities to the side and head to the spa. Sometimes it may mean that. But 90 percent of the time, self-care means doing simple, ongoing things each day that make your soul well.

One of my greatest steps of soul-care each day is to go into my office and sit in this quiet, still place with God. It's the place where I'm writing to you today. It's also one of the chilliest rooms in the house—not like my cozy, warm chair in the living room where I love to sit first thing in the morning, drink coffee, and listen to one of my favorite preacher's sermons. But because my chances of being interrupted in the living room are so much higher, since it's the hub of our house, I often gravitate back to my office, despite how cold it is, knowing I'll most likely be undisturbed there.

It does my soul good.

Other things that are daily self-care for me are using essential oils, eating healthy meals, and taking walks. Maybe for you it means lighting a candle, putting on your favorite music, or taking a hot bath. We can do things each day, despite each of our financial situations, to make and keep our souls well.

In the same way that you plan vacations, outings, and get-togethers, you need to plan your soul care too. Figure out what it's going to look like, and create a plan just for you. And don't worry, if you still need ideas on ways to make your soul well, I've got a few more for you at the end of this chapter.

Because while it's still okay not to always *be* okay, God wants you *more* than okay.

Even *happy.*

I couldn't help noticing at this stage in the childbearing challenge between Rachel and Leah, an unexpectedly sweet little moment tucked in there.

> Leah's servant Zilpah bore Jacob a second son. Then Leah said, "How happy I am! The women will call me happy."
> So she named him Asher. (Gen. 30:12–13 NIV)

In the next chapter (surprise, surprise), we'll see the comparison struggle continue. But right here, another freeing moment for Leah at the birth of her son Asher, a name that means "happy, fortunate, blessed."

Leah's okay again. In fact, she's "happy" again. I wish we could ask her exactly why, but I think it's enough simply knowing she *is* happy.

My life isn't picture-perfect at the moment. But as I look around, I see a lot of things that make me happy. Our potbellied princess pigs, for instance, who probably need to go on a diet, make me laugh every time I look at them. And the donkeys, Fred and Helen, their *hellos* (or I should say, *hee-haws*) each time I go out to the field are hysterical. Herman, the faithful pug, is always up for a walk, tug-o-war, or just a snuggle on the couch while I write. I can't help but smile. I've come a long way since that failed counseling session I told you about, where I was advised to leave my husband. (Good grief.) And now I feel more hope than despair. My soul is well again. But it's taken intentional steps. And if your soul doesn't feel that way today, hold tight. It's coming. It's going to be okay again. I promise.

～ This & That ～

Wrestle with this:

What would it take for you to be able to say your soul is well?

Remember that:

One thing I've come to understand about my soul is this: I'm the only one who can take care of it.

When it seems like God is quiet, we need to get quiet.

We can't live our lives dependent on the praise of someone else, but we can live our lives daily praising others.

Fifteen Ways to Care for Your Soul

1. Eat something refreshing. (Cucumber or watermelon are my favorites!)
2. At work, stand up from your desk every hour and stretch your arms as high as you can.
3. Do some deep breathing.
4. Make a cup of tea. Keep trying different flavors until you find one you love!
5. Wake up fifteen minutes earlier tomorrow. Use this time to pray, read your Bible, and write in your journal.
6. Drink a glass of water.
7. Take a five-minute walk.
8. Text a friend an invitation for lunch.
9. Write out a Bible verse you need right now.
10. Play a song you loved as a teenager.
11. Delete all unnecessary emails in your inbox.
12. Pick up some fresh flowers the next time you're grocery shopping.
13. Have a de-clutter session. Fill up at least one bag of items you can donate.
14. Do something new. Even if it's simple, like trying a new restaurant.
15. Turn off your phone for ten minutes, lie down, close your eyes, and just be still and silent.

Truth Four
You Didn't Do Anything Wrong

Chapter 7

It's Not Mine

When You Ask: Why Her?
Truth Four: You Didn't Do Anything Wrong

So FAR, WE'VE WORKED THROUGH three truths to the hushed *why her* question of our souls. First, we looked at the need to be honest. Second, we discovered that everybody else's picture-perfect isn't always what it seems. Then third, we admitted the need to not be okay sometimes.

And now it's time to uncover this . . .

Truth Four: You Didn't Do Anything Wrong

A few years ago, a writing opportunity presented itself that seemed to have "God's plan for me" written all over it. It wasn't something I sought out but rather was asked to apply for, which made my soul sing and dance. It was a door I was so incredibly excited about creaking open. In fact, I immediately thought this opportunity would be so great and made so much sense for me at this time in my life that it never crossed my mind to pause and pray about it.

Sometimes my brain moves faster than my brilliance.

It *didn't* feel so great, however, once I was told I'd be going up against a few of my peers for the chance of being selected for it. I knew what was coming then—the opposition of comparison. People would be listening, watching, and making decisions as they compared me against other people I knew. The whole process caused anxiety in me, and I went from feeling incredibly excited about the opportunity to feeling incredibly fearful about the potential rejection.

I did my absolute best, though, in completing the writing assignment they'd asked of all the applicants. Then a few weeks passed. Crickets. Finally one afternoon I got *the call*. The person on the line who was sharing the final decision oozed graciousness and kindness. But then she spoke the words I didn't want to hear: *"It's not yours."* The rejection rang sharply through my ears, into my heart, landing deep in my soul.

I didn't want to cry. I just sat. Silent and numb. Words left me.

So there you go. What else could I have done? I'd been compared to someone else and ultimately deemed not fit for this opportunity. And it hurt. I get so weary of people saying, "What doesn't kill us makes us stronger," because what doesn't kill us still hurts.

Despite knowing in my head I shouldn't take it so hard or jump to such upsetting conclusions, the rejection was still there. I couldn't hide it.

> What doesn't kill us still hurts.

At the same time, I didn't feel as though just forgetting about it was the healthiest option. I think we sometimes try to push our feelings aside too quickly. We don't like the pain lingering in our souls. So we shove it down. Push past it.

But we do ourselves a disservice by trying to ignore these places that stretch our souls. One day, popping up out of nowhere, we'll come face-to-face with the same person or situation that reminds us what we'd once been compared with, and an unwell soul is likely to follow. We're better off sorting carefully through our disappointments—getting *honest* about them—minimizing their power to discourage us so unexpectedly and unpredictably.

So I gave myself twenty-four hours. I took a long walk. I cleaned a lot. (Cleaning tends to be my go-to coping mechanism when life feels messy.) I wrote in my journal. And I prayed for the ache in my soul to pass.

By the next morning, I was already in a clearer head-space to spend some time reflecting on the situation. And I wrote these words to myself: "The opportunity isn't yours, but—Nicki, you didn't do anything wrong."

You didn't do anything wrong.

I wish I could tell you, once I came to this liberating conclusion, that my soul was immediately set free from the painful place I'd been wandering. In fact, when I learned who'd been selected over me for this opportunity, the dreaded *why her* question popped into my mind.

We are often our toughest critics, and learning to accept the things we cannot change is painful. But in the coming days and weeks when I would think about this opportunity, I kept repeating a short version of that statement over and over: *It's not mine, but you didn't do anything wrong.*

God was leading me to a place of surrender.

Surrender is one of those words I think we get confused. We tend to think it's a position of giving up. But godly surrender is more of a trusting God stance. Surrender isn't backing down from a desire. It's resisting the need to control things we've asked God to direct.

> Godly surrender is more of a trusting God stance.

I know most of our moms told us when we were little we could do anything and everything. But ultimately, here's the truth: we are not gifted in every area, and we are not made for everything. Not every God-assignment on this earth is ours to do. And in a world as self-centered as ours, few things are more important than embracing our awareness of this. Yes, *"it's not yours"* can be some of the hardest words your soul will ever settle into. But we have to trust God so much that if He doesn't give it to us, we don't want it.

> We have to trust God so much that if He doesn't give it to us, we don't want it.

What are you holding onto that God is gently trying to release from your grasp? Not because you did anything wrong, but simply because it's not yours?

Manipulation Mandrakes

The Bible says God blessed Leah with the ability to have children because He saw that she was unloved. Had she done anything wrong to get herself in that unloved position? Obviously not. In fact, she desperately tried to NOT be in that position. As hard as this was to deal with, she needed to accept the fact that through no fault of her own, Jacob just did not love her as much as he loved her sister. It totally stunk.

Likewise, did Rachel do anything wrong that made her unable to have children? Was it her fault that her father tricked her into having this shared relationship with Leah? No. Yet as hard as it was to deal with, she needed to accept the fact that she would always be dependent on God for her ability to become pregnant and that her marriage would always include this uncomfortable sibling complication.

But they didn't just accept it. We don't see either of these women willing to surrender to anything except their own will.

With eight sons now between them, we get a slight break in the action. But actually, it's just another episode in this ongoing comparison saga that's grown uglier by the day. Maybe you're thinking, *Can this story seriously get more ugly?* I know, I thought the same thing, but it does.

> Reuben went out during the wheat harvest and found some mandrakes in the field. When he brought them to his mother Leah, Rachel asked, "Please give me some of your son's mandrakes." (Gen. 30:14)

"Mandrakes," by the way, were plants that were believed to help with infertility.

> But Leah replied to her, "Isn't it enough that you have taken my husband? Now you also want to take my son's mandrakes?"
>
> "Well then," Rachel said, "he can sleep with you tonight in exchange for your son's mandrakes."

> When Jacob came in from the field that evening, Leah went out to meet him and said, "You must come with me, for I have hired you with my son's mandrakes." So Jacob slept with her that night. (Gen. 30:15–16)

Oh, mercy.

Here's what I hate about this. Rachel knew she had Jacob's heart. And she was fully aware this was the achiest place for Leah. Yet because she was so desperate to beat Leah not only at being the preferred wife but also at being the one who was bearing their husband's children, she grasped at these mandrakes like a miracle drug that would fulfill what God had so far withheld from her.

And then there's Leah. Always striving. Always lunging at any chance that might *(please, God, please!)* result in getting the affection from Jacob that her little sister enjoyed—anything to MAKE HIM MINE. Again, Leah hadn't done anything wrong to cause the hurt she felt from Jacob's not loving her. Nothing. But honestly, there were no words she could speak, no seductive move she could make, no beauty product she could buy to make her any more lovable or beautiful in Jacob's eyes. And even when her mandrake-purchased night with him produced yet another son to add to his growing tribe (Gen. 30:17–18), it didn't change how he felt about her.

I get it, though—this need to fight for things we desire so badly. But there is a place of freedom tucked away in this comparison compromise of the soul. And it's found in these words: *it's just not mine.*

Sister Battles

When I was a younger mom with three children under five, I consistently found myself physically and mentally exhausted. The diapers. The potty-training parties. The three meals a day. The cleaning. The refereeing of fights. Need I say more? Some days it felt impossible to find even five minutes of peace.

But one of the highlights my girls and I all looked forward to each afternoon was going out into the driveway to wait for Kris to get home. To them it was a chance to play; to me it was a chance to rest while they exhausted some outdoor energy.

I remember one afternoon, after a long day of being pushed to the limits, we went out to do our afternoon routine. I put the baby in her walker with one of those teething cookies that last for thirty minutes (cue the "Hallelujah Chorus") and told the other two to play nicely, or else. (Can I get an *amen* from the "or else" moms?)

Me? I had a folding chair calling my name and a decorating magazine begging to be looked through.

My oldest, Taylor, kept eyeing me to see if I was watching her. *Oh, I was.* She didn't understand the superpowers of a momma— how we can read magazines and watch kids at the same time. *It's talent.* To prove it, my ear was alerted within minutes to Hope and Taylor shouting about the scooter they'd brought out to play with. And because only one girl could ride it at a time, I declared as the woman in charge that for these next ten minutes, the scooter was Hope's to ride. Taylor wanted it *so badly.* But I promised her whiny voice that if she took that scooter away from Hope, the "or else" punishment was on its way.

Apparently understood and accepted, they moved on down the sidewalk—Taylor on foot, Hope on the scooter. But soon my super momma ears heard, not an *increase* in noise, but a *decrease.* (Again, talent.) I heard Taylor's voice level start to drop. She began to ask Hope if she wanted to play a game with her, a game that included Taylor being a squirrel and Hope being a bear. Satisfied that what I'd heard was a false alarm, I settled back into my magazine and took a deep sigh of relief. *Maybe my parenting was finally starting to pay off.*

But a few seconds later, I was back to questioning anything I ever did right as a mom. I heard Taylor tell Hope how their game was going to take a new twist and turn of events. "Pretend that I got hurt!" she said. "Maybe I got run over by a car. And my leg was broken. So you gave me your scooter so I could get home." Yep, it did sound a little squirrelly.

My eyes rose above the pages of the magazine, and I thought, *Don't fall for it, Hope, don't fall for it.* But sweet little three-year-old Hope Ann has always had a heart of compassion. She felt bad for Taylor, the "squirrel." Slowly, she slid off the scooter and gave it to Taylor. Then as soon as Taylor had that scooter in her hands, she began to jet down the sidewalk, leaving her sister on the side of the street alone.

I rolled my eyes, tossed my magazine down, and marched toward Taylor, shouting all kinds of get-in-time-out-now commands. With tears in her eyes, she looked back and me and said, "But I didn't *take* it. She *gave* it to me!" Yes, technically true. But only after the most manipulative move I've ever seen a five-year-old make!

Whether as little girls or grown women, we seem to naturally and easily default to taking things into our own hands. We want what we want. We want what others have. We're desperate to change things around to the way we want them to be. And probably, like with Taylor, we didn't do anything wrong to find ourselves here. It was someone else's turn. It was someone else's privilege. It was someone else's thing to do or enjoy.

It doesn't mean God's mad at you. It doesn't mean the world is against you. It just is what it is sometimes. It's not ours to take by force or to manipulate.

Secure Steps

Maybe a more adultish, more serious example will bring this all home for you.

My friend Missy was telling me about two friends of hers who were going through a battle. One friend had prayed, fasted, and spent many hours on her knees, desperate for God to bring her a husband. The other friend was married to a wonderful man but was never happy with him. Each time these two friends were together, the one who had the amazing husband would do nothing but complain about him. And her insensitivity to the woman who wanted to be a wife so much was killing their friendship.

After a few months, the married woman became separated and quickly met someone else. Less than a year after her divorce became final, she was already engaged to be remarried and was proudly announcing engagement number two to Missy—all while Missy's other friend, still on her knees, was begging God to answer this weary prayer she kept praying.

Missy said something to me on the phone that made me think about this conversation we've been having through this book. "Nicki," she said, "it's just not right. Why does God allow one person who isn't doing anything right in her life to get exactly what she wants, but the other person, who is desperately seeking God's heart every day, seems to be getting only silence from Him?"

My heart thumped a little faster. Because I wish I had the answer to God-struggles like these. The emotion Missy was feeling was raw and real, one that we've all battled from time to time. But why do we so easily default to the perspective that God blesses those who don't seem to deserve the blessing?

And why do so many of our big God-questions involve looking at other people to see what they have that we don't? Why do we jump so quickly to comparison? And if we'd ever stop ourselves from comparing, wouldn't we all be a lot closer to living more contentedly in the reality of God's sovereignty?

God is in charge. Yes. Not us. I know that's a predictably Christian thing to say, but it's true. Some would say He's "in control," meaning the same thing. But maybe, when you think about it, there's a little difference between being *in charge* and being *in control.* By saying God is in control, it doesn't mean He controls what we do. You and I both know God allows us to make our own choices and decisions. God is seeing and guiding our movements, but He is not making moves for us.

It's like how a coach tells his team exactly what to do in order to win. They're equipped, trained, and have his confidence behind them. The coach is the one in charge, but he's not in control. The players are the ones making the moves. They decide whether or not to follow his instructions, guidance, and teaching.

Here's another way to look at it. If I knew someone was about to break into my house, I would tell my daughters exactly what to do: call the police, lock the doors, and hide. If I've equipped them with everything they need and they choose not to use it, harm could soon be in their way.

In this game of comparison we play, I think it's the same way. God has given us every tool, teaching, and resource to be victorious. His Word is filled with wisdom and strategies to help us not allow our struggles to overcome us. If we don't want comparison to be something that drives our thoughts and actions, He has shown us how to combat it through the power of His Spirit. God is ultimately in charge, yes, but we choose whether to be cautious with the instructions and protection He has given us through His Word.

The reality is, we may never understand why God does what He does.

Trying to figure Him out will leave us *frustrated*.

Striving to figure Him out will leave us *fatigued*.

Working to figure Him out will leave us *faithless*.

The solution is to keep taking secure steps with God. Daily. Weekly. Monthly. Our entire lives. This process never ends. For even when circumstances look shaky, God is stable. We can believe He is securing our steps even when things don't seem to make any sense.

Is It Just Me?

Here's what I think is the bigger (and even harder) question that each of us must wrestle with at least once in our lives: "When do you give up on a desire?"

Some people will tell you, "Never!" Just keep believing God for it, trusting your answer will come if only you have a little more faith. I understand that, and I would never, ever tell you to stop believing God for something you know is from Him. Never. Our Fixer-Upper Farm is one of the most practical examples of this in my life. We knew it was ours. God had given us a dream for this property. But we almost gave up during the process of buying it because of the layers upon layers of opposition. (I share most of that journey in my book *5 Habits of a Woman Who Doesn't Quit.*)

We knew with 90-percent confidence it was ours. I mean, can we really ever say we're 100-percent sure about anything? So we pressed on until we'd exhausted all our own efforts, until there was nothing left to do but to trust God for the fulfillment of the vision He had given us.

But sometimes there's a whisper deep in our souls of something different. I can't tell you exactly how you hear this whisper. I can tell you for me, it feels like two feet firmly walking on my soul. It's not loud. It kind of aches. But it's firm. Some people call it your gut. Some call it discernment. Some say it's an inner intuition. But it's the place where we feel God saying to us—tenderly, gently, lovingly—*You didn't do anything wrong; it's just not yours.*

I've been there. I've been in those places where I'm begging for breakthrough, and all that seems to keep coming back is burden. If you were to find yourself in a place like that, I could mouth off a dozen of those easily thrown-around phrases, like: "It's just not God's timing." Or "God has another plan." Or my least favorite, "You just have to trust that if God says no, He has something better for you." I *get* all those phrases; I just don't know that I agree with their theological accuracy.

Does the time finally come when we should stop believing God for a husband? Or a baby? Or a job in a certain field? Or a ministry we've always felt we've been called to?

Again, super-hard question. Many people would never even try to answer it.

But I'm willing to gently toss one possible answer into the discussion. If we agree that God is the Creator of all, and that He formed each of us in our mothers' wombs (Ps. 139:13), doesn't that mean He also crafted our souls? He made us with desires that match His will and plan for our lives.

But many factors have influenced and shaped us since the time He formed us, including the way we grew up, the people we've surrounded ourselves with, plus dozens of other things. So chances are, we've developed desires within ourselves that may or may not be God's desires for us. Some of our desires come from Him, and some of our desires do not. As I've tried wrestling through this difficult question in my own life, I've come up with at least three signs when something I want may not be a God-desire.

Ultimately, of course, only God can show us if we should let a desire go or not. So as you read these three brief sections, know that I am *for* you, wanting you to experience all the good things He's designed just for you. But I also want you free from chasing *why her* desires that may only lead to more dissatisfaction and disappointment.

Three Signs It Might Not Be A God-Desire

Sign One: It Came from a Place of Jealousy

If you have bitter envy and selfish ambition in your heart, don't boast and deny the truth. (James 3:14)

I'm not proud to admit this, but there was a season of my life when I defined success by the type of house I lived in. After I would visit someone in a big, fancy house, I would often come home feeling so much dislike for my tiny house. I considered myself a failure because "her" home was so much better than mine. The more we surround ourselves with *perfect*, the more we feel the need to per*fect*.

But this desire didn't come from a God-given desire. It came from a place of jealousy and a messed-up perception of success.

Please know, I have absolutely nothing against big, fancy houses. They are lovely, and so are many of the people who live in them. Some people desire a big house so they can have lots of kids, which is a good desire. Or they want to be hospitable, another good desire. Or maybe they've just worked really hard and want a nice place to call home. There could be a dozen different types of good desires in this area. I'm just sharing a real and raw place from my reality. *My* desire for a nice, big house didn't come from *any* of those places.

Here's something interesting, though. The Fixer-Upper Farm is anything but a big, fancy house, yet it's everything my heart really desires in a home. Because, sure, there are things I wish looked prettier about it, or were fixed up a little more, or had better landscaping around it. And one day, hopefully, it will. But for now, this home is filled with things that make my heart smile.

Things like the simple front porch, with just enough space for two black rocking chairs. And the painted white cabinets with fun, inexpensive crystal knobs I found super-cheap online. These little details now say "home" to me. I've learned to count others' blessings while being content with my own. I quit asking God for a big, fancy house, and He changed what was most important to me about the place where I live.

What is something God might be asking you to rejoice with someone else about and yet be content with where you are?

_____

_____

_____

Sign Two: It Doesn't Line Up with the Word or Character of God

"You will seek me and find me when you search for me with all your heart." (Jer. 29:13)

The more we learn about God and His Word, the more clearly we can discern whether our wants and wishes line up with what matters most to Him. Like, if someone is in a lot of debt and they desire a new Mercedes, I'm just going to go ahead and say—this probably isn't a desire from God. Because the Bible says things like, "The borrower is a slave to the lender" (Prov. 22:7).

I know that's an easy one. But many desires that become tangled up in finances can become potentially messy in our souls. There are so many conflicting messages we hear in our culture about what we deserve and what we need in order to feel good about ourselves.

When we humbly bring our desires and lay them alongside truth, we silence all the other voices that seek to influence us. And if what we desire doesn't line up with God's Word and character, we need to ask Him to help us see it. The times I've asked Him to show me if the desire is His or mine, He's been faithful to reveal it to me.

God's character is love, mercy, kindness, justice, righteousness, holiness, and many other things His Spirit shows us as we focus on becoming more like Him. When we ask ourselves some hard questions and study the Bible, we will see what God says about the things we desire. He will do this for us, but it comes from seeking Him.

What do you need to seek God for right now?

_____

_____

_____

Sign Three: It Doesn't Make God Look Great

"Now then, stand still and see this great thing the LORD is about to do before your eyes!" (1 Sam. 12:16 NIV)

I work hard. I try to plan my days well to maximize my time. I seek wisdom. I study. I set goals. But at the end of the day, I want my desire to be that God would do through me what only He could do.

We're taught that the harder we work, the more successful we'll become. And to a certain degree, this is true. But we have to be careful who gets the glory for all the things our hard work accomplishes. Are we using it to further our comparison agenda, to look better and more successful than the people around us? Or is our desire good, wanting *God* to be seen as the true driver behind what we do?

One thing I've seen over and over again in studying the life of Jesus is that His desire was to heal the sick, raise the dead, cleanse the lepers, cast out demons, and, ultimately, to set the captives free. Amazing things. Yet as amazing as they were, He said to His disciples that they (and we) would do "even greater works than these" (John 14:12). There's a lot of discussion as to what was meant by "greater works," whether He meant quantity or actual types of miracles. But whatever Jesus did and whatever Jesus said, I want in on that. He expects us, and *invites* us, to do even "greater works" than we saw Him do.

And here's how He said this happens:

> "Don't you believe that I am in the Father, and that the
> . Father is in me? The words I say to you I do not speak on
> my own authority. Rather, it is the Father, living in me,
> who is doing his work." (John 14:10 NIV)

Even Jesus knew the work He was doing came from His Father. The closer we grow to Him, and the more we become like Him, the more we will only desire those things that more clearly reveal how our God is put on display through us.

So those are three questions I've learned to ask of my desires, even of the ones I'm having the hardest time surrendering, wondering if it's time to finally let it go.

1. Does it come from a place of jealousy?
2. Does it line up with the Word and character of God?
3. Does it make God look great?

You could probably think of more. But as we work through this process of sifting out the desires our world has put inside us versus the desires God designed us to have, here's a good, overarching question to ask: Will the fulfillment of this desire ultimately lead me (and others who know me and see me) to stand in awe of who God is?

I'll admit, even to this day when I think about that specific opportunity I mentioned at the beginning of this chapter—the one that "wasn't mine"—I feel an ache. Many times when I hear people say they surrendered a desire, a blessing quickly follows. But I'll be honest with you, there was no tangible blessing that popped up after I released this opportunity that wasn't mine. The next opportunity wasn't just "sitting there" waiting for me. It felt messy and hard.

> I can't spend my life living for a moment God asked me to surrender.

But it's not an ache that's ruining me. It's a tender place of believing that I wanted something, I ran after it hard, but it wasn't what God had for me. Maybe later down the road it *will* be my assignment, I don't know. But I can't spend my life living for a moment God asked me to surrender.

When we feel like God is blessing the woman next to us more than He's blessing us, it's easy to start to feel incredibly insecure. When things don't go the way we want them to go, our first inclination tends to be to place blame—on ourselves, on others, even on God. We can question, wonder, and even struggle with why He does what He does.

But sometimes we just need to remind ourselves that it is what it is.

Even when it's not fair. Even when *she* gets to do it or have it. Sometimes we just need to rest our souls in a position of knowing we didn't do anything to cause this hurt, loss, or disappointment we're feeling. There's a time to accept and leave it at that—all while realizing that God still has desires for us. And by seeking those (not *hers*), He can fulfill us more deeply than we ever dreamed.

～ This & That ～

Wrestle with this:

What is something you feel like God is asking you to surrender?

Remember that:

Godly surrender is more of a trusting God stance.

We have to trust God so much that if He doesn't give it to us, we don't want it.

I can't spend my life living for a moment God asked me to surrender.

Chapter 8

It's Not Fair

~

When You Ask: Why Her?
Truth Four: You Didn't Do Anything Wrong

THANK GOODNESS GOD IS NOT in the business of fighting for fair. Because if He was, there would be no Jesus. There was nothing fair about Jesus having to die on a cross to save you and me. But He did. Unfairly.

As we continue to unpack this idea that sometimes life just isn't fair, I want us to take a little pause to remember a few of the unfair situations Rachel, Leah, and Jacob have found themselves in already. These were things they didn't do anything to cause, things that were completely out of their control, yet happened anyway. Unfair things that we, even looking in from the outside at their stories all these centuries later, would say were completely unfair as well.

> Thank goodness God is not in the business of fighting for fair. Because if He was, there would be no Jesus.

To work through this, we'll shorten this phrase "You Didn't Do Anything Wrong" to #YDDAW.

First #YDDAW Situation

Jacob worked seven years for Rachel; then Laban crafted another plan for him to marry Leah, yet told him nothing about it. (Gen. 29:20, 23)

Second #YDDAW Situation

Laban used Rachel as a manipulative move to get Jacob to work longer for him. (Gen. 29:26–27)

Third #YDDAW Situation

Rachel couldn't have babies, but Leah could. (Gen. 30:1)

Fourth #YDDAW Situation

No matter how many babies Leah had, Jacob still didn't love her. (Gen. 29:34)

Fifth #YDDAW Situation

Rachel and Leah used their servant girls to one-up each other in their ongoing baby battle. (Gen. 30:3, 9)

Whew, that's a lot of unfairness happening in one story—just like there's a lot of unfairness happening in ours. And like Rachel and Leah, sometimes we keep fighting to *make* it fair. Maybe not always intentionally, but our reactions to the unfairness of life often reveal if we really believe God is fair. This struggle runs deep and wide with little or no help along the way.

Except when wisdom steps in.

Each unfair path of life offers us two options: *wisdom* or *worry*. Wisdom helps us stop spinning our wheels and constructing arguments in our heads about how unfairly we're being treated. Wisdom helps us stay focused on our lane, our assignment, and our struggles. Wisdom reveals that life is not really about you. (Or me. Or *her.*) It's always about being more and more like Jesus, who died unfairly so that we could live abundantly both here and hereafter. By applying wisdom, we're able to see beyond the current curveball that life is throwing at us.

Worry convinces us we're never going to measure up and it will always be unfair. What we need, though—instead of what worry tells us we deserve—is breathing space from our unfair comparisons. And wisdom offers us this wide-open field of confident space.

It's going to take some time until both you and I step into this space fully, but let's promise to keep fighting until we do.

Scrolling Confessions

It was late, I was tired, and I was scrolling through my Facebook feed—a potentially unhealthy scenario right there. I've found the *why her* questions rarely pop into my mind on nice seventy-degree days when I'm feeling the most confident, happy, and content. But when I'm worn down? When I'm already feeling a little lonely, unsettled, or insecure? That's when the question is just dangling there in front of me, waiting to be asked.

My finger continually swiped up on my phone screen until I came across a picture of two people I considered close friends. The three of us had recently been talking about making plans to visit a specific restaurant. And, well, *there they were*—smiling away and snapping their selfie together—*without me*, at this very restaurant.

I started to scroll again, blowing it off with an, *Oh well. I guess they thought I was busy or something.* But then my finger swiped the screen until I was back at that picture again. I stared. Looked at their smiles. Tried to see what they were eating. Checked out their cute outfits.

Then this unhealthy soul clue swept over my body, and my heart started to beat a little faster. I started to think of all the reasons why they possibly didn't invite me to come. I started to wonder, as if by emotional reflex, what I had done wrong.

Maybe they thought I was traveling.

Maybe they just wanted to spend time alone together.

Maybe they didn't think I really wanted to hang out with them.

Then came the headliner in my head. The only place these thoughts could really end up.

Maybe they don't like me.

Before I knew it, I had written quite the scenario for why I'd been left out. Whatever their reasoning, I came to the conclusion that the only thing I knew for sure in that moment was that they *weren't* thinking about me.

There's that fun word: *me*.

The *why her* struggle is really another way of saying, *"What about me?"* I don't want you thinking I'm about to start saying how you should always put yourself to the side. I'm not. But if we were to turn the word *me* into an acronym, here's what I think we'd come up with:

My desires above

Everyone else.

Pretty accurate, right?

When our desires are front and center and we experience what feels like rejection, we can become so easily offended. Offended by God. Offended by others. Offended for ourselves. But I've learned something important about all this. Being offended is not a condition inflicted on us. It's a stance we choose.

In the last chapter we looked at aligning our desires with God's desires. The more we learn to do this, the less easily offended we will be. Because when we consider the life Jesus lived, we realize how easily He could have been offended. Over and over.

> Being offended is not a condition inflicted on us. It's a stance we choose.

Jesus could have been . . .

Offended about people questioning who He was. (John 20:24–29)

Offended with people taking up His time. (Luke 8:43–48)

Offended by leaders denying His gifts. (Mark 8:11)

Offended by the betrayal and denial of those closest to Him. (Luke 22:54–62)

The list could go on and on. But whenever I see Jesus using the word *me*, it was never in a "what about me" or "look at me" kind of way. It always revolved around the bettering of someone else's life. Here are two of my favorite examples:

"Come to *me*, all of you who are weary and burdened, and I will give you rest." (Matt. 11:28, emphasis added)

"Leave the children alone, and don't try to keep them from coming to *me*, because the kingdom of heaven belongs to such as these." (Matt. 19:14, emphasis added)

> Whenever I see Jesus using the word *me*, it was never in a "what about me" or "look at me" kind of way. It always revolved around the bettering of someone else's life.

When Jesus referred to Himself—as "Me"—He was still thinking about others. And this verse confirms it.

Don't you believe that I am in the Father and the Father is in me? The words I speak to you I do not speak on my own. The Father who lives in me does his works. (John 14:10)

Even though Jesus was God, He came to this earth fully as man, aligning His desires with His Father's desires. This allowed Him to walk through many, many offensive situations without becoming offended.

And wouldn't that be a beautiful way to live today?

Especially in this age of social media?

Or should we say, *social MEdia*?

One of the main purposes of social media is to represent ourselves well. But I'm amazed by the lengths we'll go to make sure our picture is perfected. The right lighting, poses, and smiles are a must for that perfect picture post. My family is no exception to this. I've already shared some of the drama we've had over the years about pictures posted, or even the ones *not* posted. And believe me, I could tell you a lot more. Lord, have mercy.

But social media is the easiest trap of comparison because *it's there*, All. The. Time. Everyone's highlight reels are just waiting, almost begging, for us to view. The comparisons on social media have a way of leading us toward becoming easily and quickly offended.

Here are a few ways *easily offended* often starts to slip in on social media:

- Friends posting a picture of an event we weren't invited to.
- Groups created we've not been asked to be part of.
- Opinions given without being asked.
- Subliminal tweets that make us immediately wonder if they're directed at us.
- Posts we've read with a tone in our head that isn't what the writer intended.
- Bullying statements that people make behind the comfort of the screen.
- Things said that would never be said face-to-face.

Social media makes it so simple to easily offend and be offended, doesn't it? But here's what the Bible had to say about taking offense, long before social media was even a thing.

A person's insight gives him patience, and his virtue is to overlook an offense. (Prov. 19:11)

This verse is so good.

When we're engaging in a *why her* comparison—whether live, in-person, or in virtual form through social media—one of the best escape strategies comes from leaning into *insight* over *offense*. What an incredibly powerful tool. *Insight* helps us realize we didn't do anything wrong. It causes us to take a minute to step back from the situation—to exercise "patience," as this verse from Proverbs says—and see if there's anything we're missing in our assumptions.

Can you imagine how things could have been different for Rachel and Leah had they taken some time to gain insight over offense? I wonder if their hearts would have been a little softer toward one another and toward God. Maybe if they'd given each other this type of grace, they would have understood there wasn't anything wrong with either one of them. They might have even considered how God was caring for them, and caring for the other one, so personally and lovingly.

Choosing insight over offense changes the whole comparison dynamic.

Choosing Well

I'm a huge fan of podcasts. In fact, I love them so much I started my own: *Lessons From the Farm*. And when someone invites me to their podcast, I'm almost always a *yes* if I can make it work. Sure, it usually means committing almost an hour of your life. Plus, because of the length of time involved, it leaves you little room for backing out of hard conversations if things start going that direction. But overall, I love all the podcasts.

Not long ago, I agreed to be on a podcast, though I was a little unsure about it because I wasn't familiar with the person hosting the show. Still, I knew it would be a good opportunity, so I said I'd do it. But a few minutes into the discussion, I became pretty confident this interview wasn't going to be my favorite.

We began with small talk about my three daughters and my role with Proverbs 31 Ministries. But then the host started asking some questions, based on assumptions she'd made, without really even knowing me.

"So, you're a farmer's wife, correct?"

I tilted my head a little bit because no one had ever called me a "farmer's wife" before. Yes, we do live on a farm of sorts but, well . . . I just wasn't quite sure how to respond to that. *Wait, do I want to be a farmer's wife?* I thought. *What exactly defines someone as a farmer's wife?*

After I'd stumbled through that one, the interviewer laughed and continued to unpack the concept, sort of as a way of comparing me with the inspiring author Ann Voskamp. Though flattered, I could feel the discomfort rising within me. And from the way I nervously raised my hand to cover my eyes and let out as quiet of a deep breath as possible, I was glad this was a podcast and not a video interview.

Because if you've not seen pictures of Ann's farm, it's pretty dreamy. She bakes her own bread. Takes pictures in her fields with lighting that appears from the sky, which I'm pretty sure she special orders from God. [wink] Also, her husband's tractor isn't a riding lawnmower that he occasionally hijacks into a piece of farm equipment. *Not that there's anything wrong with such husbands who do things like this, ahem.* But Kris and I are first-generation farmers, which basically means we have no idea what we're doing. And as I've said, we don't call it the Fixer-Upper Farm for nothing. It's going to take a long time to get this place fully functioning.

I replied to the interviewer that I wasn't sure Ann's farm is an accurate comparison. Think more along the lines of Chevy Chase's *Funny Farm,* I told her. Yes. That's much more like it!

Still, she continued: "Do you go out to the chicken coop every morning to get your eggs for your big homemade breakfasts?"

I stared at the box of Life cereal still sitting on the kitchen counter, and thought, *I should be making breakfast now, shouldn't I?*

Oh, and by the way—mental note: we need a chicken coop.

Then the host asked, "So, you're a stay-at-home mom, right?"

Glancing at my email inbox and my long list of to-do's, I wondered how she'd gotten that impression. I guess when I told her earlier about my *work* with Proverbs 31, she apparently didn't consider ministry "work." Could that be it?

I certainly wasn't trying to distance myself from stay-at-home moms, a choice I greatly admire and value, and also a choice I made myself for many years. But in that moment, I felt this overwhelming need to justify myself. I was a *working* mom, with many assignments on my plate for the job I love. Yet I couldn't help feeling skepticism entering my heart and settling deep within my spirit. *Should I be a stay-at-home mom, not a working mom? Is it wrong that I work?*

After the first ten minutes of conversation, I realized that for the next hour I would simply be debunking this person's assumptions about my life. And while none of the assumptions were bad, they were still nothing less than that—*assumptions*—comparing me to someone or to some stereotype that was sure sounding a lot more superior at the moment to who I really am.

Can you hear the comparison talk playing in my head? Hear it writing a story about all the things I was doing wrong, and all the things I could be doing better?

But you know what? I *didn't* do anything wrong, yet comparison was convincing me otherwise. And when I finally woke up to how naturally I was slipping into easily offended mode, I made a decision to stop it dead in its tracks.

No, I'm not Ann Voskamp, and I'm okay that I'm not Ann Voskamp. She is her own one-of-a-kind person. Nor do I really know that I'd call myself a farmer's wife, and I'm okay with that too. I made up my mind, right then and there, I was going to choose *insight* over *offense*.

When we choose *insight* over *offense,* we are able to see offenders as an opportunity to become wiser.

> When we choose *insight* over *offense,* we are able to see offenders as an opportunity to become wiser.

Insight told me this interviewer probably just read a bio about me that shared about our Fixer-Upper Farm, so she assumed I was a farmer's wife. *Insight* allowed me to see this person as a person, flawed and very human, just like me. *Insight* gave me the patience to get through the interview, and while maybe it wasn't my best and I was a nervous wreck, I still came out okay.

If I would have chosen *insight* instead of *offense* that night as I was scrolling through Facebook and came across that picture of my friends at the restaurant, I could have written a totally different story in my head—one where maybe I would've had the guts to simply ask my friends why I wasn't invited, and that if they ever wanted to go to that restaurant again, I was totally in.

There's a fine balance between repressing our feelings and choosing not to be easily offended. It's not healthy for us to continue to stuff, stuff, stuff our emotions. But it's also not healthy for us to explode internally about every little thing someone says (either *to* us or *about* us) or every little thing that comes our way.

It may not be fair.

But wisdom reminds us, it's also not always our fault.

Never Say Never

There definitely have been times I *didn't* choose insight over offense. Not right away, at least.

For example, having received the invite to a particular meeting, I blocked the date off on my calendar and planned to be there. But I was given little knowledge about the context of said meeting. And I really hate walking into situations when I don't know who'll be there and what's exactly expected of me. But, you know, sometimes life requires such meetings, so I walked in anyway.

Lunches were all laid out nicely on the table, but computer screens were up, so I quickly determined this was a working lunch. I took my seat, pulled out my laptop to make sure I looked as official as everyone else. I sure didn't want to let on that I was uncomfortably clueless of my role in this meeting.

As I looked around the room and assessed the people who were there, I realized from what I knew of each person that we all had very different personalities. Which excited me, but also increased my intrigue to know more about why I was invited. Even after the person leading it talked through the agenda, I still wasn't sure what my role in the discussion would be, but the girl sitting next to me assured me there was a reason I was asked to be in the room.

After some housekeeping details, I was finally asked my opinion on a few topics and gave some honest answers. Heads nodded and lightbulbs seemed to be going off. I felt like I was connecting with everyone on a deeper level, which really gets my wheels moving and my ideas rolling. The things I had to say were seeming to be valued by everyone in the room, giving me more confidence to continue sharing.

But there was someone on the other side of the table who observed the things I was saying without ever really giving me that nod that says, "I'm *with* you." I was curious to find out why and to know his thoughts. After a few minutes, when he finally piped up, I felt like what he had to say was quite valuable as well. Truthful. But his perspective was much different than the one I'd just offered the room.

As he finished, another person began to compare what I'd been saying with what he was saying. And as the discussion continued, I could tell the room was quickly shifting toward *him*. Suddenly it was as if everything I had said became totally pointless. My words were tossed to the side like a pair of mismatched socks.

I started to wish I hadn't been invited to this meeting. I was even starting to get mad. I began to think how stupid my ideas sounded. Thoughts of inadequacy danced in my head. I wished I had just stayed quiet. This was turning into another opportunity for someone to compare what I said with what someone else said, at the same time as I was sitting RIGHT THERE. Comparison was all staring at me from uncomfortably close range. Giving me the evil eye. Waiting for the perfect opportunity to pounce its uninvited presence into my heart.

But that's comparison. Always there as an option, chasing us down, no matter how we try to get away from it.

As I got into my car to leave, my soul ached. I started making all these mental vows that I would *never* speak up in a meeting again. *Never* go to meetings for which I wasn't prepared. *Never* share my ideas.

Never again.

How typical of me. When my soul needs protection, *never* is the grand heart shield I run and hide behind. But *never* is such an awful place. *Never* is hopeless. *Never* is broken. *Never* is empty. *Never* is the connecting point between comparison and discontentment. *Never* is what comes from choosing offense over insight.

But somehow my soul made a subtle shift, choosing *insight* over *offense.*

Insight told me I had to shake this meeting off. I didn't do anything wrong. I shared my thoughts, my insights, and my opinions. Even though I felt like a loser, I could still believe in who I am and what I said—staying humble and teachable, of course, but not ashamed of the perspectives that were mine to share from my own observations, convictions, and experiences.

At the same time, *insight* told me Nicki Koziarz is not for everyone. My ideas, my opinions, and the things that make my heart beat don't mesh well with everybody on this planet. Doesn't make me wrong; just makes me normal. In fact, maybe that's a place I need to be willing to own more often. Maybe if my only desire is to get everyone to agree with me, I'm no longer trying to speak truth as I understand it; I'm simply saying what I think people want me to say.

I know we teach this generation now that they are, indeed, the greatest thing since sliced bread. We give them medals for everything; everyone is always a winner. But it's really not so in life. We don't always get to win.

Insight told me we don't always walk out of the meeting with people chanting our name and giving us a parade for being so awesome. Sometimes we take our ball and bounce it home, with no one else around to join us.

And we *never* say "never." In fact, we can be brave enough to come right back to the table the next time we're invited. And when we do, we'll show up unoffended, stronger for the insight we've gained. We'll know we didn't do anything wrong, and that we won't let comparison write a story in our hearts that we haven't authorized and approved of.

People don't need our permission to craft comparisons, but we don't have to accept the stories they choose to write. What kind of story have you been writing about yourself? About others? How has offense conspired with comparison to create lies that have become embedded in your soul?

> People don't need our permission to craft comparisons, but we don't have to accept the stories they choose to write.

Sometimes we just need someone to remind us that what we're facing isn't fair. But God is with us. And there's no need to fight for fair when His grace has already won the battle.

～ This & That ～

Wrestle with this:

What is a situation in your life where you need to choose insight over offense?

Remember that:

Whenever I see Jesus using the word "me," it was never in a "what about me" or "look at me" kind of way. It always revolved around the bettering of someone else's life.

When we choose *insight* over *offense,* we are able to see offenders as a way to become wiser.

People don't need our permission to craft comparisons, but we don't have to accept the stories they choose to write.

Truth Five

Her Gain Is Not Your Loss

Chapter 9

The Lie of Lack

When You Ask: Why Her?
Truth Five: Her Gain Is Not Your Loss

WHEN I FIRST STARTED VOLUNTEERING at Proverbs 31 Ministries, one of my first few tasks was to stuff envelopes, write cards, and do a dozen other whatever-you-need type things. I even cleaned the bathrooms from time to time. After months of volunteering, I wondered if they would ever let me answer the phones. I seriously thought it would be one of the greatest privileges of my life to do so.

And, oh boy, did they eventually let me answer the phones at Proverbs 31 Ministries!

At first, I would answer the phone with so much enthusiasm, "Thank you for calling Proverbs 31 Ministries, how may I help you?" *I was so nice.* But most of the calls we received were either a question about one of our resources or a request for prayer. And honestly, for some reason, I wasn't really great at doing either of them.

I tried my best to answer questions correctly, but I was constantly having to place people on hold so I could go find out how to respond. Even when I had the privilege of praying with someone, I felt like I prayed all the wrong things. I would sometimes get so discouraged.

Maybe I belonged back in the stuffing-envelopes, writing-cards, cleaning-the-bathroom department.

As the ministry continued to grow, the phones got busier and busier. Multiple calls would come in at the same time, and I would often drop calls while transferring them. I felt sick every single time it happened, and tried really hard to learn from my mistakes. I wanted to get better. *I should be good at this*, I kept telling myself—as good or better than anyone else.

But soon my enthusiasm for answering the phones had significantly decreased, due to the increasing fear that I would mess up. Again. Yet each time I was there at the office, I knew my role was to serve. And service sometimes looks like *service*, doing what's needed. So I faithfully answered those phones, dropped those calls, and asked for grace upon grace.

As time went on, my position grew along with the ministry, and I started to be pulled away from phone duty. Even though we each still took our turns, things were becoming so busy that we sometimes couldn't cover our rotations. That's when I suggested we make the phone team all-volunteer, comprised of people who could focus on nothing other than this important task. Yes! Everyone was excited about this solution.

Enter Kelly.

Kelly is one of the best souls I know. And she was really good on the phones too. She could answer, transfer, and respond to people faster than anyone I knew. She was also incredibly genuine, authentic, gracious, and understanding, never rolling her eyes at complaints. *[ahem]* Because Kelly was so good at what she did, eventually she was hired as staff.

One Monday morning, as I walked into the office, Kelly was sitting at the front desk, crying. I immediately stopped to ask her what was wrong and if I could help. She told me about a woman who had called for prayer that day, someone who was struggling under such a hard story that Kelly was still trying to process it. "I just feel so burdened for this woman," she said.

I knew in that moment Kelly's gifting took her to places I couldn't go.

I never cried with anyone when I prayed with them on the phone. *I* never hung up and couldn't get someone's story out of my head. This interaction made me so much more appreciative of Kelly. But it also crafted a little comparison struggle in my head. *What's wrong with me? Am I just selfish? Why do I not cry with people?*

Ugh.

I wasn't seeing something important that I needed to learn in that moment. Kelly's gift isn't my gift. My gift isn't Kelly's gift. But together, through our compatible, complementary gifts, God is able to make incredible things happen for His purpose.

Comparison's lie of lack would love for both of us to believe that the other's gift is more important, more significant, more special—that what the other person gains by exercising her gift, we somehow lose.

But that's not true. And it's why, when comparison convinces us otherwise, we need this fifth truth.

Truth Five: Her Gain Is Not Your Loss

As we look at others' callings, gifts, and talents, it's easy to assume the best things are taken, and that there's nothing good left for us. But this lie of lack leaves us missing what's right in front of us. And what a lie it is—this idea that somehow there's a shortage of assignments in heaven, that there's nothing unique in us, or that what we're good at doing isn't really good. Or that what *she* does is more valuable.

Most of the time, I think we have no idea what God has given us and what He is willing and able and wanting to do in and through us. If we're still breathing, walking, talking, moving, and thinking, there's so much more He has for us—"him who is able to do immeasurably more than all we ask or imagine, according to his power that is at work within us" (Eph. 3:20 NIV).

Think of the greatest thing you could ever do with your life. Now multiply it by the highest number you can think of. Then double it. "Immeasurably more" are two loaded words, and together they tell us what God has promised to do for us. But if we don't believe it, no one will believe it for us.

Sure, God will place people around us to cheer us on, call out our gifts, or identify our strengths. But until *we* believe it, we probably won't recognize it. We should be living in the expectation that God has filled us full of all we could ever need.

Some might call that being *prideful*; I call it being *promise-filled*.

> Pride convinces us that if someone wins, we somehow lose. But choosing to live a God-promise-filled life means believing that if *she* wins, we *all* win.

Pride convinces us that if someone wins, we somehow lose. But choosing to live a God-promise-filled life means believing that if *she* wins, we *all* win. It means holding tight to the reality that God has special assignments just for us, but also that His promises are for everyone, helping us all work *together* for a greater purpose than we could do alone.

Pride tells us God *needs* us; being promise-filled tells us God *wants* us.

Gains And Gratitude

I'm convinced one reason we struggle with a sense of lack in comparison with others stems from a lack of gratitude for what we've been given. Without gratitude, our gains in life don't last very long. Those who sustain their ability to carry out God-assignments are those who walk quietly, humbly, and with grateful confidence in what He's given them.

We see the negative side of this exchange quite often in the story of Rachel and Leah—times when God gave them something, but they never considered it enough and continued on in their greed for more.

1. Leah announced her first pregnancy with a side note that "the LORD has seen my misery" (Gen. 29:32 NIV), yet she continued to stay miserable.
2. When Rachel's servant became pregnant, she said God had "vindicated" her (Gen. 30:6), yet she remained in a place of competition.
3. Leah said God had "rewarded" her (Gen. 30:18) when she ended up pregnant, despite Rachel demanding and manipulating her way into Leah's stash of mandrakes, yet she kept feeling a lack in her life.

4. When Rachel finally became pregnant herself—with Joseph—she said, "God has taken away my disgrace" (Gen. 30:23), yet she continued to do disgraceful things.

All of these seeming gains did not last, because they didn't come from a place of gratitude. They sprouted from a place of comparison, which compromised what was really happening.

But gains announced with godly gratefulness keep growing.

Jacob, even with all his faults, was often the opposite of this grumbling attitude. He hardly lived a perfect life—especially in those sneaky dealings with his brother, Esau, and his father, Isaac. But over time, as he began to experience quite a few gains in his life, he freely gave God the credit for it—and I don't mean a little God shout-out here and there. Something had really changed in his heart. He knew without God, he was nothing, no one, and going nowhere. He knew all his gains came from the Lord.

Another time we saw this was when Rachel was blaming him for her infertility, because he got a little fired up about that whole conversation. "Give me children, or I'll die!" she said, but Jacob's wise response was, "Am in the place of God, who has kept you from having children?" (Gen. 30:1–2 NIV). He gave all the credit for all their blessings to the One who alone is able to give them.

Another example of Jacob's gratefulness toward God is seen in a conversation with Rachel and Leah about Laban. Unhappy with the way their father was treating him, Jacob began making plans to pull up stakes and strike out on his own. In order to keep things secret, he called his two wives out into the fields where he was tending his flocks to tell them what he was thinking. But he left no secret about who he was trusting to take care of him and who had been blessing him all along.

"I see that your father's attitude toward me is not what it was before, but the God of my father has been with me." (Gen. 31:5 NIV)

And then again . . .

"Your father has cheated me by changing my wages ten times. However, God has not allowed him to harm me." (Gen. 31:7 NIV)

Jacob could have turned both of these statements into gains of greediness. He could have said, "Your dad has been treating me wrong, and God will get him back for this!" But do you see the difference in his words, his tone, his heart, compared to that of the two sisters? That's why I believe Jacob's gains kept lasting, while it seems like Rachel and Leah's gains kept fading.

Gratefulness versus greediness. That's the difference.

But that's not the only difference it makes. Not only should we expect to see good things result from giving God the glory for *our* gains, we'll see even greater things happening when we start giving Him glory for the gains of *others*.

Comparison's lie of lack tries to convince us this is impossible. But a confident trust in God's promises will give us perspective to see that if others win, it does not cause us to lose.

> A confident trust in God's promises will give us perspective to see that if others win, it does not cause us to lose.

Learn, Then Live

When I got up the guts to teach my first Bible study, it came along with a new challenge—someone who was incredibly critical of how I did everything. This woman had been in many Bible studies with the best Bible study teachers, and she would sporadically drop little not-so-helpful comments about ways my class could be improved. "So-and-so did it like this," she would say, or "You should do what so-and-so did." And as insecure as I was, being new at teaching and leading, even the slightest criticism was enough to paralyze me.

Looking back on it now, I know so much of my insecurity stemmed from the rejection I faced years ago after I found out I was pregnant. To say the least, my church wasn't the most beautiful reflection of God's grace. There were painful things done and said to me by people I highly respected and loved, and even to this day sometimes it makes my soul ache when I think about it.

But the lie of lack found within comparison will also convince you that if you've ever messed up, you don't have much ahead.

So as a first-time Bible study teacher desiring to be really good, I began to copy "her"—anyone who I thought was better than me. If *she* opened her class a certain way, I felt like I needed to do the same. If *she* closed out her lesson with an activity, I concluded that I needed to do it just the same way. The lie of lack in connection with who I was as Nicki Koziarz slipped in more and more as I would look at "her," the Bible study teacher. And each time I looked, I would see how completely unqualified I was. It made me want to give up, over and over.

This did nothing, of course, but hinder my ability to trust God's goodness over the assignment He had given me to teach.

My struggle to find a godly confidence was real. I knew I had unique ideas and concepts; I knew I had things to say. But I tucked it all away for a season because of those "so-and-so" reminders. It would be years later before I would understand how much this hindered me.

This is the point in our journey together where I wish we were sitting face-to-face, drinking a cup of something warm—because I would love to hear about your journey, too, of feeling less than someone else, the way you've been listening to mine. Have you been able to see past it? Did it make you slightly numb? Did it completely paralyze you from moving forward? There's so much we could talk about.

Lies of lack can put us in such sticky situations. But you and I have the opportunity right now to grab

> When God reveals something to us, it releases a responsibility within us to do something.

hold of these things before they ruin us. When God reveals something to us, it releases a responsibility within us to do something.

As He uncovers this truth for us—how "her gain is not your loss"—let's fight for what God is doing to help both of us reach the daily deposits He has for us. Deposits of goodness, faithfulness, joy, contentment, and peace. His truth changes us, but it also cultivates us into the best "us" we can be.

Defend Her

I always wanted a sister growing up. I would dream of what it would be like to have someone with whom to share clothes, talk about boys, and do all the girly things. And while God didn't give me a sister, I think it's pretty amazing He's given me these three girls to raise as sisters.

Admittedly, I was a little clueless about this sister thing.

The confusion of the sister-struggle settled in when my oldest girls were around the ages of three and five. They could be the best of friends one minute—playing Barbies, chalk drawing, and princess dress-up. But the next minute, they could be pulling each other's hair, stealing each other's toys, and screaming about how they would NOT be inviting each other to their weddings. *At the ages of three and five!* Then approximately three minutes later, all was well again and everyone was back on the wedding guest list. This teeter-totter of confusing behavior has carried through their teenage years.

But one thing I've noticed is predictably constant. My girls have consistently defended each other like nothing I've ever seen.

Don't hate on their sister, darlin'.

Or there could be hissing involved.

And, yes, I've got a story to prove it.

My middle daughter, Hope Ann, has quite an eye for photography. In fact, until last year, she was the person who took all my headshots for promotional purposes. So to say the least, we were all really surprised when a special opportunity opened up at her school to do some photography and she wasn't selected for it.

When I found out she wasn't chosen, everything in me wanted to call that teacher to try and understand his selection process. But there are times when a momma just has to step back and let things be as they are. I've learned it typically doesn't require my involvement for everything to work out.

And Hope, undaunted, saw the rejection as an opportunity to give the cross-country team a try. *Get it, girl.*

One of her meets was during a political season. And one of the candidates in our area was using the slogan: *RUN FOREST RUN.* Cute idea for a local politician, spun off from the movie *Forrest Gump.* The slogan was divided among three different signs, each with only one word on it, stuck in the grass and spread apart on a small section of road so that you'd read them in order as you drove by. The first sign would say RUN, the second FOREST, the third RUN.

My oldest daughter, Taylor, thought it would be a good idea to "borrow" one of the signs that said "RUN" and use it to cheer on Hope for the meet. So Taylor paraded around with this bright red and white sign the whole time and got a few chuckles from fellow attendees.

After the meet was over, we were walking back to the car, deciding where to go for Hope's celebratory dinner. All of a sudden, "the teacher"—the one who'd rejected Hope's photography skills—was behind us. Hope whispered, "Ugh. There he is."

As soon as I heard it, my heart sank. *What should I do?* Frankly, I wanted to give him the evil eye so badly, but I was trying to keep it cool, so I kept my eyes straight ahead.

Hope's sisters, though, had another idea.

Kennedy had currently been in one of those quirky stages, the kind you just have to let the tweens work through. One of the things she'd been doing was practicing this horrific sound that basically sounded like a hissing cat. And she would do it constantly, especially at the most inappropriate times. So when Kennedy and Taylor realized this teacher was right behind us, I saw them whisper something to each other and begin to giggle. Then in duel-like fashion, they whipped around simultaneously.

Taylor held up the "RUN" sign, and Kennedy made her incredibly awkward and loud hissing noise.

The look in that teacher's eyes, the way he slowed his pace and looked a little bit startled for a second—I won't say I didn't enjoy it for a second.

Okay, *I know*. This is NOT appropriate behavior, and any mother should be ASHAMED for letting her kids do something like that without a SHARP reprimand. Theft of private property, disrespect for elders . . . wonder what suggestions for punishment I'll be getting in the next shame-on-you email someone sends me?

And they'd be right. The teacher had no idea what was so funny, or even what this whole ordeal was about. It had been months since his selection for the photography team. I think he honestly just thought my kids were being weird.

But the thing that brought me so much joy was seeing how my girls would go to battle for each other. Yes, they get jealous of each other and they fight like crazy, but when it comes time to defend, they are ready!

I captured a picture in my mind that day of what could help this *why her* struggle to cease. Goodness, wouldn't it be amazing if we really started to defend each other—to fight and risk in order to make others feel valued and important—so that, unlike Rachel and Leah, we would stop having to find ourselves in these incredibly sticky situations?

The more we know others are with us, the more confident we can be ourselves. Maybe that's when we'd start to see . . .

Her gain is *my* gain.

Her loss is *my* loss.

Her win is *my* win.

Her sorrow is *my* sorrow.

It would be a beautiful picture of this verse: "Rejoice with those who rejoice; weep with those who weep" (Rom. 12:15).

Pray for Her Success

One of the greatest ways to realize this truth—"Her gain is not your loss"—is to begin to pray for the women God has placed around you. And I don't mean just a little "help her Jesus" type of prayer. Picture more pounding the throne room of heaven on her behalf. And believing for the impossible in her life. And asking God to bless her in ways only He can.

Anytime the Enemy starts to slip a lie of lack in your soul as you're looking at someone who's gaining, as you're beginning to feel like you're losing, there's something you can do. Pray a "Bless Her Prayer." A "Bless Her Prayer" is powerful. It's life-giving both for her and for you. And it puts the Enemy right back where he belongs, on the sidelines. Not in the game.

Below is what I've envisioned as the "Bless Her Prayer." Insert specifics for the blanks, pray these simple words, and watch God work in strong ways, in her and in you. The lie of lack will fade as you believe the truth: *her gain is not your loss.*

The Bless Her Prayer

God, today I'm praying for _____ [insert her name]. I am grateful you have gifted her with the ability to _____ [insert her gift/opportunity]. You are a good God who gives each of us good gifts. I pray that today would be a day of increase with the ability to use those gifts in her life. Help

_____ [insert her name] to use her time, resources, and gifts wisely today. Surround her with what she needs most.

And bless her greatly.

In Jesus' name, amen.

⁓ This & That ⁓

Wrestle with this:

For whom do you need to a pray a "Bless Her Prayer"?

Remember that:

Pride convinces us that if someone wins, we somehow lose. But choosing to live a God-promise-filled life means believing that if *she* wins, we *all* win.

A confident trust in God's promises will give us perspective to see that if others win, it does not cause us to lose.

When God reveals something to us, it releases a responsibility within us to do something.

Chapter 10

Striving and Thriving

~

When You Ask: Why Her?
Truth Five: Her Gain Is Not Your Loss

WHY DID NOBODY TELL ME what would happen to my skin after the age of thirty? Ugh. This whole "reliving the teenage years through blemishes" is the worst. Add in sunspots, wrinkles, and dried-out skin, and all of a sudden you don't recognize the face in your bathroom mirror staring back at you. There's no warning either; you just wake up one day and—*boom!* There it all is.

Unlike those fun little filters on Snapchat or Instagram Stories, the mirror does not lie. Fed up with my facial woes and the mirror telling me I needed some help, I decided to pay a little visit to the beauty product store.

I was just starting to look at a few products that day when a man working there walked up to me. Before I go any further, I have nothing against men working in beauty stores. Personally, though, I felt like I needed a woman because she could understand my aging skin woes. (Let's be honest, men are clueless about these things.) But since he was the one who approached and asked if I'd like some help, I didn't want to be rude. So I told Cosmetics

Man what I needed. The basic need? Make my face look normal again.

He pulled out brushes, foundations, powders, and all the tricks of his trade. But even after trying multiple products, nothing seemed to satisfy his master makeover on me. He would look at me with this face of dissatisfaction that really wasn't helping my already insecure blotchy-face situation.

Finally, apparently stumped, he took a step back and asked, "Are you drinking enough water? How many hours of sleep are you getting? Are you stressed out?" I started to roll my eyes. I needed him to fix my *face*, not give me a therapy session. I just wanted whatever made those women in the magazines have such flawless skin—and, if it's not too much trouble, maybe throw in whatever allows them to live the kind of life where they can drink enough water, get enough sleep, and not be so stressed out.

The reality is, beauty is one of the main areas where we as women start to feel inferior to each other. We will do drastic things, including emptying our bank accounts on products with a promise, just so we don't have to feel inferior. Cosmetic companies know this about us because they spend billions of dollars each year on advertisements to make us believe their product will help us look just like *her* . . . or better. I read a statistic that one of the top cosmetic companies in America spent 8.3 billion dollars in ONE YEAR on advertisements.

Whoever said you can't put a price on beauty was apparently misinformed.

But we don't have to take the bait. Continuing to work through this fifth truth—"Her gain is not your loss"—reminds me of a quote from Eleanor Roosevelt: "No one can make you feel inferior without your consent." *No one.* Not advertisers. Not

Pinterest. Not social media. Not the woman next to you. *No one* can make you feel inferior. Feeling inferior is something you choose.

But I get it, because insecurity can make this a very complicated struggle. For years we've been encouraged through various campaigns to be our own brand of beautiful. But how do we even begin to do this when the world is constantly telling us what beautiful is?

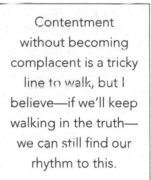

Contentment without becoming complacent is a tricky line to walk, but I believe—if we'll keep walking in the truth— we can still find our rhythm to this.

I think it all goes back to gaining a greater understanding of what it really means to "win"—with our jobs, our relationships, our beauty, or whatever else is making us feel like we're losing. Contentment without becoming complacent is a tricky line to walk, but I believe—if we'll keep walking in the truth—we can still find our rhythm to this.

Hidden Idols

Idols are both visible and invisible. For me, having a flawless face became a visible idol. Which stemmed from a comparison I made. I was willing to spend a lot of money to become a better version of myself. But sometimes, the idols in our lives are hidden.

We saw in the last chapter that Jacob finally had enough of the Laban mistreatment. He had done his time, worked hard, and was ready to be free of sharing his time, energy, and success with his scheming father-in-law.

So while Laban was off tending to his sheep for a few days, Jacob jumped on the opportunity to load up his wives, children, animals, and possessions and roll out of town. But what Jacob didn't know is that they were leaving with something else in their luggage.

> When Laban had gone to shear his sheep, Rachel stole her father's household idols. (Gen. 31:19)

Idols. Commentaries tell us these idols were small and portable, and Rachel probably stole them because she thought they would bring her protection and blessing. Or perhaps she wanted to have something to tangibly worship on the long journey ahead. We don't know for sure. It seems, though, the lie of lack deep inside her was what led her to do such a crazy-desperate thing.

Laban was sure to find out about this, of course. And as soon as he was notified that Jacob had fled with his family, he took off after him. When he finally caught up with them and got to where he could speak to Jacob, Laban wasn't exactly happy to see them:

> "What have you done? You have deceived me and taken my daughters away like prisoners of war! Why did you secretly flee from me, deceive me, and not tell me? I would have sent you away with joy and singing, with tambourines and lyres, but you didn't even let me kiss my grandchildren and my daughters. You have acted foolishly. I could do you great harm, but last night the God of your father said to me: 'Watch yourself! Don't say anything to Jacob, either good or bad.' Now you have gone off because you long for your father's family—but why have you stolen my gods?" (Gen. 31:26–30)

Jacob hadn't stolen *anything*. And he was so sure that neither he nor anyone in his family could have done such a thing, he confidently shot back at Laban, "If you find your gods with anyone here, he will not live! Before our relatives, point out anything that is yours and take it" (Gen. 31:32)—having no idea that Rachel, the love of his life, was the one at fault.

So Laban went around from tent to tent looking for the idols. What happened next? It's pretty funny. Get ready.

First he marched into Leah's tent, searching high and low. *No idols.* Then he stormed into Rachel's tent, where she was sitting *on the idols,* which she'd hidden in some sort of saddlebag.

Now watch this . . .

> She said to her father, "Don't be angry, my lord, that I cannot stand up in your presence; I am having my period." (Gen. 31:35)

Stop it. *She did it, y'all!* She pulled the female excuse card. And it worked! Laban walked right out.

But just because Laban couldn't see his idols in her tent doesn't mean we can't learn something from Rachel again. The striving never stopped. The fight to win never ended. This constant tug-of-war in her soul—the one that led her to lie and steal—would convince her to do *anything* to come out on top.

It's an example of caution for you and me. Whatever becomes an idol in our hearts can convince us to do things like max out our credit cards on beauty products, tell a little white lie to get out of trouble, or put everything at risk, just to get what we think we want. Rachel didn't know it, but her life was actually on the line.

There is so much at stake with this comparison struggle. But for every idol we uncover, it's one less thing we're becoming enslaved to. And that makes all this so worth it.

Striving Thoughts

I wish I could tap into the thought process of Rachel and this idol-stealing. But because I know a woman's heart, I know that sometimes things just get tangled in there. It's messy. It's complicated. We get desperate and we do desperate things. But the untangling of our souls always begins in our thoughts.

Whatever is making us feel threatened needs to know that desperation will no longer be our decision-making driver. When I think about the things that God *does* want us to strive toward, there are so many good things.

There are plenty of God-assignments to go around. He's not running out of opportunities for us to partner with Him in a unique way with our own skill sets. After all, there are still many, many hurting, lost, and lonely people in this world. There are dreams still to be dreamed. Buildings still to be built. Words still to be written. Kids still to be adopted. Art still to be drawn. Businesses still to begin. The list goes on and on and on.

> While dozens of things can try making you feel inferior to the woman ahead of you, your God-assignment doesn't have to be one of them.

So while dozens of things can try making you feel inferior to the woman ahead of you, your God-assignment doesn't have to be one of them.

I struggle when people hold their assignments from God with a tight grip, as though He would entrust no one else but them with it. Imagine how dull and boring this world would be if there was only one worship leader, one author, one teacher, one pastor, one artist, or one architect.

We'd only have a few good words to read, a few songs to sing, a few sermons to listen to, a few pictures to look at, and a few buildings to admire, without much variety. But God doesn't put a limit on how many people are allowed to do things important to His purpose. There's room for all of us to take our place, without feeling restricted or rejected or replaced in the shadows of everyone else.

> God doesn't put a limit on how many people are allowed to do things important to His purpose.

As I'm typing these words, I'm thinking of a woman who was driving me back to the airport after a meeting where I'd been teaching. I recognized she was in comparison mode right away. One after another the questions came— about ministry, book writing, and running a farm. She told me she wanted some advice on a few of her God-assignments, which I was happy to offer from anything I'd learned.

But it felt like it was turning into one of those conversations where the other person seems to have an end goal of making themselves look busier than you. She would ask me a question, but before I had a chance to respond, she would ask *another* question that would ultimately lead to her telling me something about herself. On and on it went. I couldn't tell if what she really wanted was advice or if she just wanted me to know all *she* was doing and planned on doing with her life.

The whole conversation left me feeling empty. Sad. Because this constantly striving, constantly trying to stay ahead, constantly trying to impress and justify ourselves leaves such a hollow place in a woman's soul.

The desire to succeed, of course, is a great goal. In fact, I don't see anywhere in the Bible that doesn't encourage us to work toward success. But we need to be careful that all our striving doesn't (1) mask our insecurity in success, or (2) lead us away from thriving in the season we're currently living.

When my girls were little, someone gave me some really good advice: "Nicki, don't ever wish a season away." Like, don't say, "I wish she would hurry up and walk and talk and feed herself." I took that advice, always trying to embrace each season. And now as their childhood seems to be fading more and more each day, I find myself still trying to embrace every season, every step, every moment.

It doesn't mean I don't have days when I'm driving through four different carlines/drop-offs and fantasizing about the day when I no longer have to do this. Or wondering what I'll do when I finally have my nights to myself, with no kids to scoot here or scoot there. But instead of wishing this or that away, let's learn to embrace the place we're in today.

> Strive toward what's ahead, but learn to thrive in the season you're currently in.

Strive toward what's ahead, but learn to thrive in the season you're currently in.

Sometimes when I read the Bible, I fail to remember there are a million other stories that happened which were never told.

I'm feeling this reality as we're learning Rachel and Leah's story because so far all we've seen is ugly, ugly, and more ugly.

But there *had* to have been some good moments. After all, you cannot be around children very long without them doing *something* to make you smile. And there are a lot of babies in this story. Surely at least one of them had to do something cute once in a while!

Another thing I wonder: How did Rachel and Leah feel toward each other's babies? A lot of sisters I know who have babies close in age do everything together. And they love the other's baby as if he was their own. Do you think they experienced this at all? Or do you think, instead, all they could see when they looked at each other was loss? Hate? Pride? Distrust? Did they miss the goodness of God looking up at them each day?

When a woman struggles to understand the goodness of God in her life, she will always look at the success of another woman as a threat to her success.

> When a woman struggles to understand the goodness of God in her life, she will always look at the success of another woman as a threat to her success.

Listen, just like Rachel and Leah, God's goodness is surrounding you. Even if it feels like everyone else is winning and you're losing, the goodness of God is at work in you because the goodness of God is at work in *all* His kids.

God is crazy about who you are and the plans He has for your life. Even in the midst of your messy, He is still crazy-grace-filled-in-love with you.

So go ahead and take this verse I mentioned earlier that the psalmist prayed, and believe it for your life too.

> Surely your goodness and love will follow me all the days of my life, and I will dwell in the house of the LORD forever. (Ps. 23:6 NIV)

I don't know all the reasons why it feels so hard to see the goodness of God in our lives. I don't know why we're often only able to see it in others. I just know if we're not careful to stay in the reality of God's love and goodness, we'll slip into a place where our souls become unwell and we'll miss what's right in front of us.

She Did It Better

I had been invited to a pretty swanky party. The kind where the men wear black ties, the finger food is too fancy to be called finger food, and they even valet park your car. Excited as I was to attend, I was also slightly nervous.

I wasn't sure how to dress appropriately, how to act, or if I even knew how to valet park. Throughout the day I texted other friends to compare outfits, ask insecure questions, and see who was going to be there. But when it was time for the party, my nerves were getting the best of me.

The valet ordeal was complicated to me, so I just parked my own car. I didn't know who to talk to, where to sit, stand, or even set my water glass.

I felt so out of place.

Whenever we host people at our farm, it's more of a flip-flops and hamburgers and hot dogs vibe. I want to be fancy, but I'm just not that good at fancy.

Driving home that night, those little sounds of comparison started thumping through my head. *Would I ever have a party that included valet parking? Was my insecurity evident? Was I dressed appropriately? What if they found out I didn't use the valet, even though it was already paid for?* The entire way home, comparison was trying to convince my soul that there was something wrong with me.

Finally I took a deep breath and told myself, "Fancy is just not who you are. That's who *she* is. But it doesn't make you right and her wrong."

Or to put it in the words of the five truths we've explored so far . . .

1. You need to be honest.
2. See it like it really is.
3. You don't always have to be okay.
4. Sometimes you didn't do anything wrong.
5. Her gain is not your loss.

The truthful answer is, her party was fabulous. (I'm being honest and seeing it like it really is.) I felt insecure (I don't always have to be okay), but I can say with pretty confident assurance that I won't ever have a party that fancy. (I didn't do anything wrong though.) But it doesn't make *her gain* of a great party *my loss*.

There are a dozen other scenarios you and I could work through to grasp this same concept, to apply this truth to our lives. What is it about *her* that makes you feel the most inferior right now? And what is it about God's plans and purposes for *you* that should make you feel content?

We have to find contentment with who we are without becoming complacent in who we are becoming.

In the next two chapters, I'm going to help you move to that place, to true peace.

But before we get there, consider doing three things:

> We have to find contentment with who we are without becoming complacent in who we are becoming.

1. Decide who or what is rivaling the peace in your life.
2. Open your Bible or use a Bible app or website to look up verses on peace and contentment. Write down at least one. Memorize it. Tell a friend about it. And make it part of your daily thinking.
3. Go back and pray the "Bless Her Prayer" any time you start to feel inferior the next few days. Keep track of how you feel before, during, and afterward.

～ This & That ～

Wrestle with this:

What might be a hidden idol of comparison in your life?

Remember that:

While dozens of things can try making you feel inferior to the woman ahead of you, your God-assignment doesn't have to be one of them.

God doesn't put a limit on how many people are allowed to do things important to His purpose.

We have to find contentment with who we are without becoming complacent in who we are becoming.

Truth Six
Let the Success of
Others Encourage, Not
Discourage You

Chapter 11

You Be You

~

When You Ask: Why Her?
Truth Six: Let the Success of Others Encourage,
        Not Discourage You

I ONCE HAD TO HAVE a semi-hard conversation with a friend. The reason I say it was semi-hard is because this friend and I have the kind of relationship where we can say what we need to say and move on. But still, this one wasn't fun.

She was struggling because someone had started a business similar to hers. And this other person had a good following, was building a respected reputation in the industry, and showed decent potential for her business to thrive.

My friend admittedly felt threatened.

But she didn't just *feel* threatened, she started *acting* threatened.

Each time we talked, I sensed more defeat and desperation in her voice than the time before, as she verbally weighed all the possibilities of what could happen with this new business scenario. And the longer this went on, the more often her roller coaster of emotions began riding on jealousy. Whenever she would say something about this new business owner, I would take a deep breath, waiting to feel my stomach twist and turn. I knew I needed to say something, but I didn't want to hurt her already fragile spirit.

Finally one afternoon, while we were on the phone discussing things, I gently walked her through all the reasons why her business was awesome. I reassured her that I was in her corner, that I truly believed in *her*, in her talent, and in her ideas. But then I said

> You gotta let her be her and you be you.

something really hard about this spirit of competition she felt with the other person: "You gotta let her be her and you be you. You are both called and chosen to do this assignment. Not either/or. But this anxiety you feel? It has the potential to ruin you."

I don't think it's what she wanted me to say in that moment, but it's what she needed to hear. Know how I know? Because I needed someone to say it to me years ago when I walked through a similar situation. I let being threatened by someone else's success ruin days and weeks of my life. And it took what seemed like forever to get over it.

Here's the thing I'd say to you if you were in a situation like this, where the comparison was controlling you. I know what *she* is doing looks really awesome. And *she* makes it look effortless. Maybe *she* can actually do it better. But *she* is called, chosen, and set apart by God for a purpose. *Hers.*

And so are you. For *yours.*

God's purpose isn't a battlefield for competition. It's a safe haven of calling.

Instead of letting this *why her* struggle become a rivalry game, we can instead choose to use the energy it generates and turn it into something that actually benefits us. Her *and* us. Because believe it or not, it's really possible for comparison to become a good thing. A healthy thing.

Spiritually, it begins where all good things begin—in the presence of God. In order to see the goodness of God in our lives, we need the presence of God. Because the presence of God is what keeps us humble.

Humility is the by-product of God's presence flowing in our lives.

When we are in His presence through studying His Word, worshiping, serving, and being around others who love Him, He gives us a humble, healthy confidence. This comes only from Him, the confidence of knowing He's created us to do something great with our lives. His presence whispers assurance over our souls, even when we feel the most vulnerable.

> God's purpose isn't a battlefield for competition. It's a safe haven of calling.

His presence gives us the ability to keep walking in His favor while cheering on that girl next to us, regardless of how threatened we feel. By staying in His continual presence, we learn that our God-given gifts and talents are not for making ourselves better than the woman next to us. In fact, we learn to value what *she's* doing more than what *we're* doing.

> Humility is the by-product of God's presence flowing in our lives.

Do nothing from selfish ambition or conceit, but in humility count others more significant than yourselves. (Phil. 2:3 ESV)

I realize this is hard to do. It takes guts to release your insecurities to God and confidently be yourself while watching someone else live out their dream (especially in places where it looks like *your* dream). But it's more than possible. Great favor and blessing flows from being a cheerleader of God's women.

That's why we need a final truth to anchor this journey we're making through comparison:

Truth Six: Let the Success of Others Encourage, Not Discourage You

Everyone has something to teach us. Sometimes it's who we want to become and sometimes it's who we never want to become. This truth is powerful because it helps us glance but not glare. It guides us to a posture of learning rather than following.

Keep the Struggle Factual

I'm a bottom-line type of girl. Sure, I love a good story, but for the real things in life, I want the cold, hard facts. No fluff. Just facts.

Have you ever heard of something called an Oreo conversation? It's where you start off with a compliment, get to the hard facts, and then end with another compliment. I used to think this was such a nice way to tell someone something hard. But oh mercy, how I hate it now. If I start to feel like someone is about to Oreo me, I want to run.

Just tell me what I did wrong, and let's move on. When dealing with comparison, there's nothing better you can do than get to the facts, because the facts may actually help you. The fluff is where we get it all messed up in our heads.

Fluff is the pretty, perfected side of something we see. We throw fluff around on the Internet all day long. All we see is the finished product: the perfectly painted room, the date night extravaganza, the night out with the girls, or the vacation that makes others drool. Fluff hinders us. Only the facts can change us.

So the next time you're facing comparison, here's something I want you to do. It's a practical tool you can pull out to help take control of what comparison can do to your mind. It will help keep the facts front and center. We'll call it the comparison solution. *A math problem of sorts.* Here's what it looks like:

Compare + Compliment + Calculate the Cost = Take Control of Comparison

In order to unpack this, I want us to look at three different scenarios.

Scenario One

First, let's imagine a situation similar to the one my friend was going through. Perhaps you really desire to become a business owner. For years you've paid attention to small businesses, but you've never pulled the trigger on your own. Fear of failure often haunts you. But one day you run into an old friend. As you're catching up on each other's lives, she shares with you that she has started the exact business you were thinking about starting. At first you feel a little threatened, but instead of settling into the *why her, why not me, that's not fair* mentality, you take back control of comparison by sorting through the solution.

Example of what you could say: "That is so interesting you started this business because I've tossed around that same idea before." [Compare] "You are so smart, I'd love to learn anything I can from you!" [Compliment] "What gave you the courage to get started? What are some of the struggles you've had? What's a piece of advice you'd give someone who wants to start a business?" [Calculate the Cost]

Most people want to share with others what they've learned. It makes them feel smart! By asking her questions from a genuine heart free of comparison, just wanting to learn, you might get all kinds of secrets from her that you hadn't thought of.

Scenario Two

You've been on Pinterest for weeks drooling over a kitchen remodel you want to do. All the right ideas are pinned, and you're ready to activate them in your own kitchen. But one day when you're attending a committee meeting in someone's home you've never been inside before—lo and behold, your dream kitchen is in *her* house. Instead of letting your eyes turn green, however, you compliment her and ask the right questions.

Example of what you could say: "This is the kitchen of my dreams." [Compare] "Everything in this room is stunning!" [Compliment] "Can you tell me how you painted your cabinets? Where you purchased your handles? And what paint color this is?" [Calculate the Cost]

Yes, use her success as a learning tool, not a comparison weapon. If you do, I'm confident you'll start to understand what it would really take for you to have that dream kitchen instead of feeling bad for yourself. Pinterest will tell you it's so simple and affordable, but we've all beheld the lies of Pinterest. Take those facts you gather from her, and figure out your own plan.

Scenario Three

What's the first question we always ask someone after they lose weight? "How'd you do it?" Right? But what we're *really* asking is: "Is it possible for me to do what you did?" So the next time you run into someone who's accomplished a physical goal you also desire, instead of letting comparison tempt you into thinking it's not possible for you, put it through the comparison solution.

Example of what you could say: You think, *Goodness, she looks great.* [**Compare**] "I think it is so amazing what you've accomplished!" [**Compliment**] "Can you help me understand how you had the determination to stick it through? What were some of the tools you used? What was your biggest obstacle?" [**Calculate the Cost**]

I know it might seem silly to put your comparisons through this filter and solution, but I promise, if you can just remember these three words—*Compare, Compliment,* and *Calculate*—they will help you sort through any comparison situation and keep the facts front and center.

Learn to ask the right questions, and you will let the success of others encourage, not discourage you.

> Learn to ask the right questions, and you will let the success of others encourage, not discourage you.

Become someone who seeks success instead of sulking over failure. Remember, if it's possible for her, it's also possible for you. But let the right things—the facts—be what fuel you, not the need to be the best or do better than *her*. All those other things will only lead you to a place of internal conflict.

Was That What You Wanted?

If we don't learn to keep comparison struggles in healthy, humble, *her*-honoring ways, they will never stop messing us up. If we spend our lives *chasing* other people rather than *cheering* and *championing* other people, we'll just be left empty.

So my heart is kind of achy as we go back to Rachel and Leah's story. I'm not incredibly excited to tell you what happens.

The last we saw of them, they had hit the road with Jacob and their children. Then Laban had caught up with them, upset that they'd left, and accused them of stealing his household idols. After Rachel's time-of-the-month distraction had kept the idols from being discovered, Jacob was fed up with Laban—twenty years' worth of mad at the way he'd been mis-

> If we spend our lives *chasing* other people rather than *cheering* and *championing* other people, we'll just be left empty.

treated. But let's give these two old rivals credit. Even with all their issues vented and exposed, they made an uneasy peace. Laban headed home, but not before blessing everyone. Even Leah. Even Rachel (Gen. 31:36–55).

You could wonder if this might be a nice place for a reset in their relationship. They're out on their own now. A little older. A little wiser? Ready to lay down their differences and stop fighting so hard? It could seem this would be the place we start to wrap a pretty little bow around the story. Laban and Jacob are friends again. Jacob is off on his own. And everyone has babies now.

But after a couple of key events in Genesis 32–34, the Bible says Rachel became pregnant a second time. Years earlier—back when Leah was having all the babies—Rachel had said to Jacob, "Give me sons, or I will die!" (Gen. 30:1). This desperation of not measuring up had made her not even want to live if she continued to see herself as falling behind as a wife and mother. And then read what happens . . .

> When they were still some distance from Ephrath, Rachel began to give birth, and her labor was difficult. During her difficult labor, the midwife said to her, "Don't be afraid, for you have another son." With her last breath—for she was dying—she named him Ben-oni, but his father called him Benjamin. So Rachel died and was buried on the way to Ephrath (that is, Bethlehem). (Gen. 35:16–19)

Have you ever seen someone slip into eternity who didn't live a life reconciled with the ones they loved? My grandfather was a kind soul, but he had a lot of broken relationships as he left this earth. It was hard to watch his passing unfold, but now, from those of us left here, there's a lot of wrestling with the "whys" and "what-ifs" and "wonder what could have been different." I've never lost someone to death who was close to me and not wished for more time, more connection, or more understanding of their soul.

So I find myself wondering what Leah's thoughts were like at that moment. We don't hear anything from her at this point in the Scripture, but we know she's there. What was she thinking? Feeling? Grieving? Desperately wanting to say?

The other day, we were celebrating my dad's birthday by enjoying a meal together with him and my family. At some point during the festivities, my youngest daughter, Kennedy Grace, was asking him all kinds of questions about *his* dad, her great-grand-father, who passed away about eleven years ago.

I have such great memories of him, my grandfather. Like how he wouldn't call me Nicki, only Nickel. And the way he wore his socks up to his knees. His only mission each day seemed to be reading the paper in the morning, then shooting his BB gun at squirrels that were trying to get into his attic. And his favorite know-it-all phrase to prove someone wrong—I can still hear it in my head, spoken in his Michigan accent—was, "I don't think so."

I thought I knew exactly who my grandfather was. Ralph Chevalier. I knew he'd been in the military and worked at a car plant for most of his life. But Lord have mercy, I apparently knew nothing about this man.

My dad started filling Kennedy in on all kinds of things I'd never heard and never thought to ask. Just little things, like, um . . . how he helped build NUCLEAR WEAPONS. *What?!* Yes, and he was an illegal immigrant to the United States. *What?!* The more my dad spoke, the more my mouth just dropped.

That night I was filled with so much regret because I never really took the time to get to know my grandfather. I had fun with him. I spent time with him. But there's such a difference between knowing someone and knowing who they are. And we will always be less than we can be if we don't learn to truly value them.

I don't know the specific regrets that lay beside Rachel's death-bed. I don't know if Leah felt foolish for wasting so much time being incredibly bitter with her. I don't know her thoughts at that moment. The only thing I'm pretty sure of is this:

She was no longer thinking, *Why her?*

What I've Learned from You

One of the wisest things we can do in life is to learn from other people. Everyone has something to teach us. I know it takes time to get to know them. It takes effort. It takes work.

But if we'll dial back the comparison impulse long enough to treasure and tap into the beauty of those around us, we can discover some amazing things. In fact, by not focusing so much on *her* as a competitor but rather on *her* as a person, *her* life can actually help motivate me beyond my own complacency.

Part of what happens when I let her success encourage me, not discourage me, is this: I discover *myself.*

I find out who I really am.

Here's what I mean by that. Whenever I see myself primarily in terms of my comparison with others, I tend to downgrade myself to my labels, titles, and affiliations, the places where I think of myself as competing (and often not measuring up). *Wife. Mom. Speaker. Author. Proverbs 31 Ministries.* But do I really know who I am—who Nicki Koziarz is—without all these words attached to my name? If one or more of these things were ever taken away from me, who would I be?

> By not focusing so much on *her* as a competitor but rather on *her* as a person, *her* life can actually help motivate me beyond my own complacency.

It's crucial that I stop turning my life into a performance to be graded in terms of how it compares with others. Instead, I need to be serving and listening and learning from others so that I can become freer to live for God in the ways He's uniquely made me—serving Him *through* my various titles and responsibilities but not being *defined* by them.

Yet maybe, like me, you haven't taken much time in life to think about who you are. Sure, you've done the icebreakers at parties, Bible studies, and work settings that help you get to know other people in the room, to find the common threads that build community. But you haven't used that kind of information to weave the threads together that give you a truer understanding of who you are as an individual.

- What makes you smile?
- What makes you cry?
- Where do you find yourself challenged by God?
- What are the things you want to do with your life that you don't need anyone else to see?

If we're constantly comparing, we never unpack the answers to questions like these. We spend our entire lives in the shadow of everyone around us—getting to know *them*, all while wondering who we are. Getting rid of the comparison filter is what enables us to do both—learn more about *others*, while also learning more about *ourselves*.

I have a sign hanging in my living room created by The House of Belonging, a company that makes the most beautiful hand-lettered art. It's the perfect reminder of this truth:

Darling,
That one thing that you have that nobody else has is you.
Your Voice. Your Story. Your Vision. Your Heart. Your Soul.
So laugh and sing. Dance and play. Write and draw.
Create and build. Love and shine. Stay true to yourself.
Embrace your inner beauty and remember to live life
AS ONLY YOU CAN.

Almost daily as I pass by this sign, I pause and wonder, *Am I living life as only I can?* If my answer is yes, I press on. If my answer is no, I linger at the sign a little longer.

Because you are the only you. And goodness, that's a beautiful fact. Maybe I can learn that from you, and you can learn it from me. Then instead of being competitors, we are learning to live as women who complement each other.

> Instead of being competitors, we are learning to live as women who complement each other.

~ This & That ~

Wrestle with this:

What are the things about your life that make you, you?

Remember that:

God's purpose isn't a battlefield for competition. It's a safe haven of calling.

Learn to ask the right questions, and you will let the success of others encourage, not discourage you.

By not focusing so much on *her* as a competitor but rather on *her* as a person, *her* life can actually help motivate me beyond my own complacency.

Chapter 12

It's Different

When You Ask: Why Her?
Truth Six: Let the Success of Others Encourage,
    Not Discourage You

I'M A BIG FAN OF retreats.

My friend Yvette once asked me to join her for a retreat at a place called Apple Hill. I was so excited to go there because I'd heard that God had done some incredible things in the lives of others at this retreat lodge. I believe we can meet God anywhere, of course—in the carpool lane, at the grocery store, sitting in our living room. But there's something really special when we pull ourselves away from the rest of the world, just to hear from Him.

We invited a couple of other friends to come along, then packed up my Goldfish cracker-infested minivan and headed that way. When we arrived, we settled into our rooms. The lodge was buzzing with excitement. Everyone had come with so much expectation about what God was going to do while we were there! We were so excited.

We kicked off our weekend by climbing up this mountain called Prayer Mountain, where the Moravians (a tight-knit group of Christians known for their extraordinary devotion to prayer and world missions, especially in the first centuries following the Protestant Reformation) had once held a twenty-four-hour prayer vigil. Miraculous, humanly unexplainable things have happened on this mountain.

We worshiped, we prayed, and indeed, some amazing things started happening.

One of the women walked off into the woods and found a rock that bore the very word she had chosen as her word for the year. Another person received a phone call while she was there, delivering really good news she was waiting to hear. Everyone seemed to be having these remarkable encounters with God. Yet there I was, waiting, hoping, lifting my eyes shyly up to the sky, saying to God, "Hey, I'm here too."

As I drifted off to sleep that night, I whispered in my soul, "Lord, I really want to have an encounter with You. Please meet me here."

The next morning I woke up quite early, way before anyone else, and I felt this desire to go back to the place where we had been praying the day before. Only this time I went alone. It was cold, so I bundled up in layers and began making my way up the mountain.

When I got to the top, I set my Bible and my journal down on a bench and put my headphones in. I began to have an amazing time of worship. Many, many ideas came to my mind, verses to read. It was a really powerful experience. I felt like I was hearing God speak in a way I'd never heard before. But after about an hour into this amazing time of seeking Him, I sensed something rather startling in my spirit, as if I was being told to *get off this mountain—NOW!*

At first I shrugged it off. Probably it was just an internal sense of fear, something strange like that. But then a few seconds later I felt it again.

Get off this mountain—NOW!

I quickly gathered up my things and started to *run* down the mountain as fast as I could. The whole time I was running, a million thoughts were swarming through my head.

Am I crazy?!

What on earth is happening?

Did God really just kick me off His mountain?

I opened the cabin door and ran straight up to my room, where my friend Yvette was blow-drying her hair. My face must have been white as a ghost because she looked at me with big eyes and said, "Nicki! What's wrong?"

I began to tell her about what had happened, and her eyes kept getting bigger and bigger. "Nicki, I've been to this place a dozen times, and I've never heard of something happening like this. God does powerful things here, but I bet no one's ever gotten kicked off the mountain before!"

After we'd talked a while, I went downstairs by myself to try journaling my thoughts, plopping down in this big overstuffed chair next to the fireplace. I needed some clarity. This was crazy. One of the other ladies from our retreat was sitting on the couch across from me, and I was just about to start writing in my journal when this big man walked into the room carrying a huge coffee pot. Setting it down heavily on the table, he said to my friend, "Hey, were you the woman who was up on the mountain this morning?"

She shook her head. "No, that was *her*," she said, nodding at me.

I sank into my seat. I thought for sure it was about to come. God's wrath, being announced to all the world through this rough-hewn mountain man—some kind of divine insight he'd received on why God had told me I wasn't welcome in His presence on that mountain.

He looked firmly at me and said, "Well, it's a good thing you got off that mountain when you did! There was a coyote chasing you!"

What?!

I suppose I should've been struck with fear—you know, the delayed feeling that comes from realizing how close to death or danger you might have come. But instead I felt an intense relief, knowing God hadn't actually kicked me off His mountain! I ran upstairs to tell Yvette, and we laughed until our bellies hurt.

So, yes, I'd had my encounter with God.

But good grief, it sure didn't look like anyone else's. And this is my caution for us as we take a last look at this sixth truth—"Let the success of others encourage, not discourage you." Let them *encourage*, not *discourage*. Conquering what comparison can do to your soul is going to look different for you than it will for the woman beside you. We can obviously learn much value from her successes, and we should seek to appreciate and celebrate what makes her able to do it. But God wants to set us free from this idea that our journey must look a certain way in order to be real and authentic.

> Conquering what comparison can do to your soul is going to look different for you than it will for the woman beside you.

That day, on that mountain, when God allowed my journey to look different than everyone else's on our retreat, I was set free from some important things that had been holding me back.

Free from the fear I'd been wrongly carrying, the one that said my whole life had been a disappointment to Him, especially whenever things didn't turn out like I thought they should have.

Free from the fear that hearing God's voice and sensing His movement in our lives is what He does for special people, not for everyone else, not for me.

Free from the fear that my encounters with Him, if they were real and genuine, should look like other people's, not unique to me, different.

This retreat was a shifting point in my journey. It made me realize just how one-of-a-kind and different God wants all of us to be. He wants us to be united, yes, but He also wants us to thrive as individuals, without all these over-analyzed insecurities.

Maybe this is your shifting point in your journey. Right here. Right now.

What Is Freedom?

I think our Christian culture has tossed the word *freedom* around with very little explanation. We sing songs about being free and how Jesus gives us freedom, but do we really understand what it means to be free?

Does it mean having a house as clean as *hers*? Is that freedom? Even if it comes at the cost of yelling at the kids all the time and making everyone miserable?

Does it mean having a wardrobe as beautiful and trendy as *hers*? Is that freedom? Even if it comes at the cost of debt and maxed-out credit cards?

Does it mean having sales numbers higher than *hers*? Is that freedom? Even if it comes at the cost of sacrificing big chunks of your family time, your health, your sanity?

> Freedom means stepping into the middle of your story, changing it not to look like *her* but to look like what you believe God has envisioned for *you*.

Freedom means stepping into the middle of your story, changing it not to look like *her* but to look like what you believe God has envisioned for *you*.

When Jacob lost his beloved Rachel during childbirth, he heard the name she pronounced over her final child—Ben-oni—a name meaning "son of sorrow." I can picture Jacob holding his baby boy in his arms, tears streaming down his face, whispering the name his wife had given their son as she slipped into eternity. Ben-oni. Ben-oni. Ben-oni. "Son of my sorrow."

But, no. Mmh-mm. No way was this child going to represent sorrow his whole life long. No way was he going to carry a legacy of loss into his much brighter future.

[Rachel] named him Ben-oni, but his father called him Benjamin. (Gen. 35:18)

Benjamin—"right-hand son," a son of honor and strength and possibility, free to be what God would go on to do with him and with his descendants throughout the history of His people.

Freedom gives us the grace to keep believing the Lord for good even in the midst of sorrow, even when our experience feels less than what others are seeing. Freedom says we can win, not in *spite* of or in *place* of how others are winning, but in ways that assure us God is working His will through us with purpose and personality—a unique journey with Him that is truly incomparable. And refreshingly free.

What Is Greatness?

The times when we lack *freedom* and ask "Why her?" are probably because we're wrestling with a lack of recognition, notice, or attention. A lack of *greatness*. We see others who are doing great, enjoying great marriages, raising great kids, engaged in great things—as if everything they touch in their lives turns to *great*. I get why people say things like, "Oh *they* are the next Michael Jordan, Billy Graham, or Joanna Gaines." What they are saying is, "I see greatness in them." But it's a greatness based on a comparison to a celebrity-type person.

But I think we need to define *greatness*.

Because if to me, *great* means I'm up, made my bed today, and didn't yell at any of my kids, that may just need to be my great for this morning. If *great* means I travel to the other side of the world and spend weeks in poverty-stricken situations, helping those who cannot help themselves, that may be what's great and spells success for me.

Success is defined in the eyes of the beholder. So who are you letting behold your success?

I've found one of the best ways to keep comparison from controlling me is to stay totally focused on what God is doing in and through me, because what *He* determines to be great is a lot more important than anyone else's interpretation of it.

Is greatness an impossible standard set by the world? Is it some picture you drew on a paper as a child? I'm not about to tell you to stop striving for success. We all need success in our lives. But don't expect your greatness to be defined (or limited!) by what it looks like on others.

> Success is defined in the eyes of the beholder. So who are you letting behold your success?

And never expect your greatness to come easily. We have assignments in our lives, and no one is going to do them for us. And most days the fulfillment of these assignments won't involve a Netflix marathon or hanging out on Facebook all day. It's hard, focused work. But working on your assignment is one of the best things you'll ever do. And it will keep comparison at bay.

There's an ultimate goal for each of us today: More and more like Jesus. Less and less like anyone else.

> There's an ultimate goal for each of us today: More and more like Jesus. Less and less like anyone else.

I don't want to be you. You don't want to be me. There are things I'm sure I'd love about your life, and there are things I'm sure you'd love about mine (specifically Fred the donkey, because you should want a Fred in your life). *[wink]* But I promise you, if our shoes were swapped just for a day, you'd want your life back.

The common thread we share, though, is the need to look more and more like Jesus. All of us. No one is exempt to this need.

The more okay we become with ourselves and with God's expression of greatness in our lives, the less and less we'll ask the *why her* question. Because when you are so busy working on yourself, you don't have time to be worried about what anyone else is doing. I know this isn't what social media tells us. It sucks us in, day in and day out. But here's what I'd say: just don't let it.

Don't.

Turn your phone off, close out your computer tabs, and fall in love with your life again.

The other day my middle daughter, Hope Ann, said something to me that made me think about this idea of loving our lives. While scrolling through her social media feed, she said, "Mom, I don't think anyone would ever want to put us on a TV show. Our life is pretty boring."

Boring? Really? Good grief, I can't remember the last time I said, "Hmm, I'm so bored today, what shall I do?" So I looked with her at her phone and quickly clued in to her uninteresting life perspective. She was looking at a picture of her friend who was off on an amazing adventure in Colorado. Yeah, life on the Fixer-Upper Farm, where her chore for the day was scooping up poop in the barnyard—I see how that could sound pretty *boring* compared to

> Someone once said, "Don't compare your chapter two with someone else's chapter twelve."

skiing in Colorado. But we often forget how great our life is because we're always looking at someone else's "better" life.

Someone once said, "Don't compare your chapter two with someone else's chapter twelve."

Be careful not to look at the end of someone's story and think it just somehow ended up great. There was a process to get there. Things they had to learn along the way. Hard work that had to be done. Remember this as you learn from *their* great.

But ultimately, don't let anyone else's *great* be your *great.*

Out of the Shadows

One of the first Bible studies I ever completed was *Esther* by Beth Moore. She unpacks several concepts around the idea that it's tough to be a woman. The one statement that spoke to me the most during this time was: "It's tough being a woman in another woman's shadow."

This statement struck me so hard because I came across this study during a season when I was learning to understand what it means to lead. I was in quite a few women's shadows. Some I enjoyed learning from, but for others, I couldn't wait to step out of their shadow. It was like Mrs. Beth totally understood this season I was in. You have to be there, but it's tough.

I believe every leader teaches us one of two things: (1) the way we'll choose to treat others, or (2) the way we'll *never* treat others.

One of the leaders I served under at that time was teaching me more about the second of these two options. She made me consistently feel less-than. Sometimes I wondered if it was because of my story. Other times I wondered if it was my age. I even wrestled with whether or not she just thought I was unqualified to lead.

Whatever it was, she was extremely critical of everything I did and never seemed pleased with my efforts. It was really hard to stay put in that season and not run in another direction. But when my season of serving under this leader came to an end, I walked away convicted, determined never to make another woman feel like she didn't measure up in my presence. I never wanted to cast that kind of shadow.

But even good, encouraging leaders can cast a shadow of sorts. And if we're following them—if we're often comparing ourselves to them, seeking to emulate them, wondering if we'll ever be like them—even *their* shadow can become a bit suffocating and restricting. What started out as learning can turn into leaning. Leaning on her words. Leaning on her ideas. Leaning less and less on Jesus and more on *her.*

There's one thing I've learned about these shadows. Most likely, no one put you in this shadow but yourself. And in another woman's shadow, you will always stay in her steps, which is why there comes a time to move.

Learn what you can learn. But don't stay there.

If you're feeling a lack of freedom right now—if you're feeling unsatisfied by the assignment God has given you—if you're feeling a drain on your confidence that's limiting what you know you should be becoming—it might be time to step out of *her* shadow.

And as you step out, step forward with a holy confidence. You may not always get this thing right, but you know how to be more and more like Jesus. I promise you, you do. It's in there. Dig down deep. Seek Him more than anyone or anything else. And you will find yourself in the shadow of His presence . . . the only shadow we should really remain in.

Protect me as the pupil of your eye; hide me in the shadow of your wings. (Ps. 17:8)

Settled but Never Settling

A few months after this book is published, I'll be helping that not-so-little-anymore pink bundle of goodness pack her stuff for college. My heart can't even contain the emotions I feel about it all. My eyes are getting pretty leaky as I write these last few thoughts.

They say the days are long and the years are short, but it's felt like it's all been short.

Being Taylor's mom the last seventeen years hasn't been perfect. In fact, it's been more messy than beautiful. I know I'll still be her mom, of course, as she swoops off into adulthood. But there's something special about the journey I've had in raising her. She's taught me the greatest lesson of my life: learning to become the mom she needed. And with every great lesson comes highs and lows.

I feel a deep joy in knowing we didn't just survive this season of life. We've thrived. I suppose one of the benefits of being a young mom sending a kid off to college before the age of forty is that I feel like I've still got a lot of life left in me. Yet there's also sadness in knowing what I know now about comparison, because it stole so many moments of joy from me. And like with Rachel and Leah, those are moments I can't go back and change.

But I know comparison no longer defines me, and I pray it won't define Taylor either. Or my other two girls. Or you. My past felt broken for a very long time, but I've moved on. It's time for you to move on, too, my friend. From this moment on, you are not the same.

Together we've embraced these truths:

1. You need to be honest.
2. See it like it really is.
3. You don't always have to be okay.
4. Sometimes you didn't do anything wrong.
5. Her gain is not your loss.
6. Let the success of others encourage, not discourage you.

And just as Jacob turned his son's name around, it's time to turn this thing around too.

As my life has gone on, and I've stopped looking to the left and the right and been able to see what's directly in front of me, I love what I see. Yes, the reflection in the mirror has a few more wrinkles and a few circles under her eyes, but her spark is back. She's exactly where she's supposed to be. And life is turning out the way it should: *Messy. Beautiful. Challenging. Changing.*

So I'm settled. But I'm not settling.

God is still working, writing, and walking me through this story. I don't know what else God has for you, but I know it's more than you can imagine. And I pray this book has given you a fresh glimpse of it.

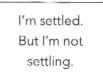

I'm settled. But I'm not settling.

Never settle for the seed of comparison, my friend. You are more than this. You are way more than anyone could ever compare you to. I love you, and I believe the best days are still ahead for both of our lives.

Until we meet again . . .

Nicki.

∿ This & That ∿

Wrestle with this:

What does it mean in your life to say you're settled but never settling?

Remember that:

Conquering what comparison can do to your soul is going to look different for you than it will for the woman beside you.

Freedom means stepping into the middle of your story, changing it not to look like *her* but to look like what you believe God has envisioned for *you*.

Success is defined in the eyes of the beholder. So who are you letting behold your success?

Proverbs 31 Ministries

If you were inspired by *Why Her?* and desire to deepen your own personal relationship with Jesus Christ, I encourage you to connect with Proverbs 31 Ministries.

Proverbs 31 Ministries exists to be a trusted friend who will take you by the hand and walk by your side, leading you one step closer to the heart of God through:

- Free online daily devotions
- First 5 app
- Daily radio program
- Books and resources
- Online Bible Studies
- COMPEL Writers Training: www.CompelTraining.com

To learn more about Proverbs 31 Ministries call 877-731-4663 or visit www.Proverbs31.org.

Proverbs 31 Ministries
630 Team Rd., Suite 100
Matthews, NC 28105
www.Proverbs31.org